How to Be Your Own
STOCKBROKER

CHARLES SCHWAB

A DELL TRADE PAPERBACK

A DELL TRADE PAPERBACK
Published by
Dell Publishing
a division of
Bantam Doubleday Dell Publishing Group, Inc.
1540 Broadway
New York, New York 10036

The chart on pages 38–39, "Stock Market History since 1926," is reprinted with the kind permission of the Standard & Poor's Corporation.

ISBN: 0-440-53865-3

Reprinted by arrangement with Macmillan Publishing Company

Printed in the United States of America

September 1986

20 19 18 17 16 15 14 13 12 11

MV

How to Be Your Own STOCKBROKER

CHARLES SCHWAB

"Schwab's advice is good—often excellent. . . . It goes far beyond opinions to provide careful, well thought-out analyses of various investment vehicles, of opportunities and pitfalls, and of ways individuals can indeed do things on their own."
—*The Miami Herald*

"Schwab's book guides you through the market maze, and when he's led you to the center, you'll be much more comfortable making those decisions . . . without having to pay [that extra 75 percent] to someone who will hold your hand."
—*Philadelphia Daily News*

"A provocative and instructive investment guide."
—*Publishers Weekly*

"Blessedly free of Wall Street jingo. . . . A clear, plain manual for the first-time investor."
—*Daily News* (New York)

"Lots of hints about investing [or not investing] in metals, futures, puts and calls, mutual funds, even real estate."
—*The Seattle Times*

"Ranges over a wide variety of investments in a down-to-earth, highly readable style."
—*D & B Reports*

"The book is an honest one, pretty well living up to its title and going beyond, offering sound and tested advice about the stock market."
—*Sun-Times* (Chicago)

Contents

Acknowledgment

With deep appreciation, I want to acknowledge the superb writing and editorial skills of my friend William Proctor.

1

Why You Should Do It Yourself

An era of good news for the everyday investor and his timid cousin, the would-be investor, has finally arrived. From staid State Street in Boston to bustling Wall Street in New York and clear across the country to the Pacific Stock Exchange there has been a revolution—no other word for it—in financial services. A radical change has occurred in *who* now sells you stocks, bonds, insurance, and other forms of investments, and in *how* they are sold and delivered. And the change is definitely for the better.

Today any investor can be truly independent—independent of unfair, bloated commissions and of the self-serving broker whose "advice" is tainted. The sordid fact is that the riskier the investment that a broker "advises," the higher is his own take. For example, as we'll see in more detail later, a broker will get considerably more for selling you a piece of an extremely speculative wildcat oil exploration deal than he will for getting you to buy an equal amount of some blue chip stock.

I'm reminded of an eager-beaver stock salesman I knew in Florida who took a prospect to the harbor at Palm Beach. As they surveyed the various luxury craft floating before them, the salesman pointed out all the yachts owned by successful brokers.

"But where are the customers' yachts?" the prospect innocently inquired.

The fellows who still own most of the yachts—the brokers, specialists, deal makers, investment bankers—have made a profitable priesthood out of dispensing their words of alleged wisdom. But I don't accept that wisdom. The blunt fact is that, for his or her best long-term interests, the investor will be most successful by really knowing what to do and by *making his or her own decisions*.

It's as simple as buying a car. Suppose your old jalopy has been giving you trouble, and you decide that the time has finally arrived to trade it in. If you walk into an auto agency to seek guidance, what will you get? Exactly. The shiniest, newest model, replete with the most expensive accessories. And it won't necessarily work any better than your old car, which may just need a new part that you can buy for a couple of hundred dollars.

So it is with investing. If investors don't know what they're looking for, only one lucky fellow in 1,000 will stumble on an honest guiding light from among the priesthood. The other 999 had better start thinking for themselves to protect their financial health. Otherwise, when they reach their sixties, they'll be very unhealthy, financially speaking: in a word, almost broke and largely relying on Social Security, and you know where Social Security is probably going—or, rather, isn't going.

This book is not intended for those sad sacks who fear life, change, and taking a chance. They are the hide-under-the-bed disciples of "disaster daddy" Howard Ruff, or of gloom-and-doomer Eliot Janeway, or of the "gold bugs."

Rather, I'm writing for those upbeat, optimistic Americans who are looking confidently toward the long-term growth of the United States and who want a piece of the action. But even if the spirit is willing, the head may be weak. You go to grammar school, high school, and probably college, and along the line, while you learned many interesting things about ancient Greece, you didn't learn a single thing about handling your own finances. I know I didn't, and I attended one of the finest institutions in the country.

But managing your own finances is more important—infinitely more important—than ever before. In the old days only the husband worked, and little capital was created except for the house and lot that families managed to acquire. But the past few decades, despite problems with inflation and recession, have seen an encouraging set of developments, namely, many Americans have been able to make and save some money.

At the same time, through the establishment of IRAs and Keoghs and through various public pronouncements, the government has been sending us frantic signals: "Save money for yourself because we feds won't take care of you completely."

You don't have much choice: You, and no one else but you, must take care of yourself. But how?

The first step is to recognize the many biases in this investing business.

More than six decades ago independent investment counseling began because, even then, wealthy individuals detected a conflict of interest on the part of their brokers. The more stocks those brokers peddled, the more commissions they raked in. Ironically, the riskier the investment they touted, the higher the commission they were allowed to charge.

Even banks, those marble pillars of rectitude, were charged with overreaching with their clients. These alleged abuses led to the passage of the Glass-Steagall Act of 1933, which separated commercial banking from investment banking. Sometimes they recommended the purchase of issues in which they were also the underwriters—or those issues guaranteed the financial support of certain securities. Moreover, when an issue underwritten by a bank was a lemon, they might have tucked some of it into their trust accounts. What widow or orphan could possibly have known the difference?

I mention the problems of the past only to underscore the unhappy fact that whenever your money is involved, somebody else is scheming to get some of it, something that has not changed over time.

Now, I know what some of you are thinking: "You, too, Chuck Schwab, want some of my do-re-mi, don't you?" Actually, I do, but not on the usual terms. As a discount broker I welcome one and all as customers, especially the "fat cats" among you. Five percent of our clients provide 50 percent of our revenues. Of course, we need the other 95 percent of our customers to provide a stable revenue and to make us truly a large-scale, profitable company, but remember: A discount broker makes money not by rolling up excessively high commissions from a small number of well-heeled clients. Rather, we concentrate on providing a large number of customers with low, competitive rates.

The discount brokerage business is important in the financial revolution we've been talking about. So let me give you a thumbnail sketch of our experience during the past decade or so to illustrate where independent, do-it-yourself investing has come from—and where it may be going.

We started in 1971 as a small, lightly financed company. Three years later we got our feet wet in offering commission discounts when the Securities and Exchange Commission (SEC) fixed a trial period for discounts on very large and very small transactions.

Then came May Day in 1975, a truly devastating May Day for the traditional, button-down clique of high-priced brokers. On that day the SEC mandated an end to all fixed commissions, and the way was paved, in gold, for the advent of the independent investor.

The pious hope of the government regulators had been that competitive rates would result in lower rates for all investors. But old-fashioned greed nixed that dream. The big stock-buying institutions, such as the mutual funds and pension funds, used their muscle to negotiate inordinately deep discounts for themselves, leaving the brokerage houses short of some of the commission cream they had been accustomed to savoring.

So, they recouped by gouging the little guy. Except for a few large and vocal investors, individual customers were hit with higher rates than ever before. Since the big day of deregulation, the brokerage firms have raised rates again on many occasions to offset the loss of institutional revenues and to pay for a galaxy of unrelated, and often unneeded and unwanted, auxiliary services.

By raising their rates sky-high, the big brokerage houses may have temporarily pulled in a little extra cash, but they also, unintentionally, raised a large umbrella under which the burgeoning discount houses could operate. Through streamlined operations and the wizardry of computer technology, a few of the discounters have reduced the buying and selling of almost anything to a phone call.

Also, instead of huckstering, commissioned stock sellers, we have hired only *salaried* brokers and thus eliminated any temptation to churn accounts and hike commissions. Since discount brokerage houses don't directly share the revenue from commissions with their brokers, they have been able to reduce drastically the size of their commissions. In fact, our commissions are as much as 75 percent below those of the full-commission firms.

Our experience has proven that there is, indeed, a strong and growing body of independent investors who want to control their own financial future. Many of them, we've found, don't need broker research. They use independent sources of information, make their own decisions, and come out better than those timid fellows who think they need their hands held by a big firm's broker.

Also, many of these investors are downright afraid of broker guidance, and rightly so. They perceive correctly that many ordinary brokers are victims of moral schizophrenia. Since ordinary brokers make their living on commission revenues, their advice has to be less than fully objective. (That's putting it as politely as I can.)

The discount brokerage firms found themselves riding the wave of the future. The big brokerage houses continued, unwisely, to raise their commission rates. And investors kept coming to us in increasing numbers, eager to learn how they could save even more on transactions. We soon found ourselves basking in an environment where deregulation and discounting, on everything from liquor to airline tickets, were becoming more accepted and expected.

But it hasn't been all champagne and roses. Far from it! When you take the big boys on, you have to expect some repercussions, and we got plenty of them.

Back in 1975, when we wanted to join one of the stock exchanges, I had to appear several times before its ethics committee. That group was preoccupied with the exchange's "know your customer" rule, under which the broker is obliged to know an investor's personal circumstances. For example, supposedly, if a misguided fellow wants to buy inappropriate securities for his portfolio, the broker can say, "Tut, tut, friend. This is not right for you."

In plain fact, though, the rule is used to help a broker judge whether a customer can pay his bills. The rule was used against us on the theory that we wouldn't necessarily know the "appropriateness" of the customer's investment choice. So we had to get down in the trenches and fight—successfully in the end. But the big-brother-knows-best insolence of that rule still galls me. Who is some stockbroker to tell you, a person of majority age with a decent credit record, what you may or may not buy?

That kind of thinking came out of the hothouse, club environment dominating the exchanges for more than a century. In my opinion—and it's now an opinion that's grudgingly but widely accepted—an investor should be able to come to a firm like ours and buy anything he pleases!

But this "know your customer" rule wasn't the worst of our problems. More important, the major firms employed the rankest discrimination against us. They might have the plum position in an office building, on the ground floor or mezzanine, but like spoiled kids they would threaten to break their leases if we were allowed a puny thousand square feet way up on the twentieth or thirtieth floor.

This happened to us in Seattle, in Phoenix, and in Chicago. In one instance I resolved the problem over a weekend, but only by calling for help from the U.S. Justice Department.

Another time I testified before a federal grand jury in Washington on behalf of another discount firm that did "$2 business" on the floor of the New York Stock Exchange. They had been specialists and floor brokers, who charged only $2 per 100 shares to help execute some of the excess business of the big houses. But then, as creative American entrepreneurs are wont to do, they decided to take things a step further. They entered the discount business, and that very same day every bit of their $2 business was canceled. Total, rank discrimination! Some people might call it competition, but I say it's economic oppression.

Don't misunderstand me, I'm not crying the blues for myself or my firm. From a few thousand clients back in 1975, we now have over 1.2 million. We have branches all over the country, and even in Hong Kong, so there is the sweet smell of success about our still-growing organization. But I do get a little heated up when I sense a corporate bully trying to block a legitimate enterprise, especially when that enterprise is trying to make things easier and less expensive for the small investor.

Despite efforts to slow or halt the growth of discount broker-age houses promoting the cause of the independent investor, there arc probably about a hundred discount firms in the country now. Even some eight hundred of our banks now offer discount bro-kerage, and in a year or so I expect to find two thousand banks in the brokerage business. About 25 percent of retail brokerage business is presently transacted by discount firms, up from 6 per-cent three years ago. And some authorities predict the figure will grow to 25 or 33 percent of the industry in the next few years.

The services available these days with discount brokers can enable you to "do it yourself" in the fullest sense of that term— and do it at a much lower price than through the large high-com-mission houses. Here are just a few of the privileges that a top-level discounter should be able to give to you, the independent investor:

- Savings of up to 75 percent on your commissions for trading in most investments, including New York and American Stock Exchange listed securities, listed options, over-the-counter stocks, and corporate bonds.
- An advanced computer system that speeds transactions and access to account information.
- Twenty-four-hour, seven-days-a-week service for investors who want to place orders, and for answering customer inquiries.
- An "all-in-one" asset management account, with market inter-

est rates on cash balances, low-cost brokerage, competitive borrowing rates, free national debit cards, and free check-writing privileges.
- A no-fee, flexible, self-directed Individual Retirement Account (IRA).
- A comprehensive system for purchasing no-load mutual funds.
- Offices throughout the country to give you in-person access to your accounts almost anywhere you may live or travel, be it Kansas City, St. Louis, or San Francisco. Most investors want proximity to their financial service company—definitely within the same state, and hopefully at least in the major city of that particular state.
- A toll-free 800 number to enable you to keep in touch with your account at no cost.
- Ticker-tape and quote machines with instantaneous stock price changes. Within the next couple of years some discounters will be setting up an on-line quote operation whereby any telephone in the country can be used as a quote system or to gain access to information about your account. Or you'll be able to use your own computer to plug into this information.

It's possible to get some or all of these services with a discount broker; at Schwab we offer all of them, and that's more than most high-commission houses can say. But, then, quite frankly, I'm personally more oriented toward the individual investor than toward the stockbroker. In fact, it may seem a curious thing, but I've never even been a stockbroker. Except for founding and running our discount firm, I've spent most of my time on *your* side of the fence, as an individual investor. I've used all the major firms and their brokers, and those experiences have given me complete empathy with the investors and what they want and need.

In short, I know that the savvy, independent investor mostly wants a haven, a refuge from the aggressive, commission-obsessed broker; and that's what discounters have given them. You can hide from the world if you like and manage your holdings at a very low cost, without any high-pressure distraction by securities salespeople. The amount you'll save on commissions can go right back into your portfolio, and your net worth will increase just that much more rapidly. Also, you'll get a lot more fun and satisfaction out of life.

In a nutshell, many advantages are available to the investor who wants to manage his own investments. But, obviously, the would-be independent investor must learn to gather information, evaluate that information, and apply basic money-management principles before he can really succeed. To help him or her achieve this end, here are the topics we'll consider in some detail in the following pages:

How you can learn from the successes and mistakes of others. In particular, I'll devote considerable space to some of my own crises, failures, and triumphs so that you can profit from a little hindsight.

How the stock exchanges work. It's important to have a feel for where your money goes, from the time it leaves your hands until it goes into your chosen investment vehicle.

More practical details on the differences between discount and regular stockbrokers. An absolutely essential point for aspiring do-it-yourself investors.

Basic principles of successful investing. You should understand concepts like diversification, ways to divorce your emotions from the pressures of daily trading, and the pitfalls of rigidity. Being too rigid spoiled one of the best possible trades of my life—because of a measly ⅛ of a point.

The psychology of the markets. The various investment markets are rooted more in mass psychology than in logical analysis. Also, the markets move in recognizable cycles. The sooner you understand how this works, the faster your portfolio will grow.

Ways to evaluate the worth of a company and its stock. This requires more common sense than an expertise in higher math.

The "life cycle" program for effective investing. How your age and circumstances should determine the appropriate balance of your portfolio.

The gobbledygook of corporate publications. You'll get a once-over-lightly understanding of the prospectus, annual report, and financial statement. They really aren't as formidable as they may seem.

How to use the popular financial press. Obviously, you should do some reading, including books, magazines, and newspapers that deal with investments. I'll suggest the most helpful publications.

The basic investment vehicles. These include the "classic" securities and techniques, like stocks, bonds, put and call options.

Keys to the mutual fund maze. The important differences between load and no-load mutual funds, as well as some guidelines on how to choose the most promising funds.

The money market funds. These liquid, interest-bearing investments enable you to "park" your money while you're waiting for another type of investment, or they may be a good long-term deal in themselves. We'll discuss how safe they are and the relative merits of these funds as opposed to bank savings accounts, which are backed by government insurance.

The relative benefits of real estate. How to assess the value of real estate as an inflation hedge, and the possible drawbacks of tying up your money indefinitely in real property. Also, some comments on REITs (real estate investment trusts).

A look at the "treasure-chest" investments. Precious metals, such as gold, silver, and platinum, diamonds, and other valuable items and collectibles have caught the fancy of various investors at certain stages of the economic cycle. But there are dangers as well as possible benefits to this approach. A related investment, even more hazardous, is the commodities market: Approach with caution!

Tax shelters. These have become a couple of come-hither buzzwords in recent years. But before you leap, it's important to look closely. Some checklists and guidelines will be provided.

Individual Retirement Accounts (IRAs). Every investor should have one, but some types of funds and securities are better than others. An IRA is a good tax shelter in that you get a deduction for the amount you contribute in the year of your contribution, and also the taxes on the interest, dividends, and capital gains are deferred until you withdraw the money from the plan. But you have to choose your IRA investments wisely: An IRA plan is only as good as the investments it shields from immediate taxation.

How to solve the margin mystery. Because of past abuses by unwary investors, margin buying has acquired an unfair image. Actually, using the line of credit that it offers at a relatively low interest rate is an attractive proposition. Of course, as with any use of debt, you must proceed carefully. So how much debt on margin can you prudently carry? What are the best investment uses for margin loans?

How you can be sure your investments are safe. There are a couple of aspects to investing that your regular, high-commission stockbroker will delicately avoid, if he can get away with it. So many banks and brokerage houses have been sending out SOS messages—or actually going under—that you can be rightly concerned over the safety of your life savings. So we'll explore such questions as: Is it wise to entrust your stocks and bonds to brokerage houses? How about using the major depository institutions? Are discount brokers as safe as the full-commission houses?

The importance of family involvement in investing. I strongly urge that you make the entire family—including your preteens—part of your investment process. Bringing in the children will compensate for the shocking lack of personal-finance teaching in their schools.

Allow me for a moment to act as a family, rather than financial, counselor. I strongly urge the spouse more knowledgeable about investing, whether male or female, to bring his or her partner into the planning sessions and explain how the markets work. The result will be greater family financial security, as well as better understanding and communication among family members.

Finally, the steps to becoming an investment sage. When you've mastered the basics, a period of experience in applying those principles will help you develop into a real expert on your own finances. Instead of relying on tips, like a besotted horseplayer, instead of a lamblike acceptance of a broker's questionable advice, you'll find you've achieved at least four virtues: patience, philosophical discipline, a commitment to systematic study, and a rigorous rein on your emotions.

But to reach this final plateau it's necessary to get out into the real world and make your own mistakes, as I've made mine. And that brings me to the first major topic I want to explore, the importance of learning from the experience of more seasoned investors in developing your own personal do-it-yourself strategies.

2

How I Learned to Ride
the Investment Roller Coaster

For every big success a person has, there must be at least one or more huge failures. I think that's a basic law of the universe recognized by most highly successful independent investors. I know it has certainly applied to me.

In the late 1960s I was riding high on a lifetime roller coaster that was bound to head down at some point. It all started in 1967 when associates and I established a no-load mutual fund called Investment Indicators.

For those new to the investment game, a mutual fund is an investment company that buys shares of stock or other securities in a variety of corporations. Investors who hold shares of the mutual fund automatically achieve the safety of a diversified portfolio, without having to buy shares of many separate companies. Our fund was *open-ended* in that it sold its shares directly to the general public, without the necessity of having *fixed capitalization*. That is, we could issue additional shares as new investors asked to buy them. A *no-load* fund is one which doesn't charge a commission or sales fee on purchase.

From a zero start in our Investment Indicators fund, we quickly reached significant success, eventually achieving a fund with assets of $20 million. It was probably the largest fund of its kind at that time in California.

But then the bottom fell out.

The problem started in the home of the shoot-out and face-down, the great state of Texas. A number of Texas residents had invested with us by sending their money through the mails to California. But the Texas state government soon notified us that we had to "cease and desist" taking any shareholders from that state until we filed special Texas registration forms.

Well, that was something of a pain, but we acquiesced. However, Texas wasn't through with us yet. You see, the bureaucrats added the following zinger: "Before we can allow you to register, you must offer *rescission* to all your present Texas shareholders."

That's an ugly word, *rescission*. It meant we'd have to give Texas investors the unlimited right to cancel all their transactions. In short, we would have had to refund their money, plus 6 percent interest, *at the price they had paid originally*. In other words, all the risk would be on us and none on our investors, a sure-fire deal for the investor as long as the fund can stay in business. Unfortunately, staying in business then became our main problem.

The concept of rescission dates back to the old "blue-sky laws" preceding World War I. These laws were laudably designed to protect innocent investors from unscrupulous hawks in the financial world. But applying those statutes to us was not only unfair, it was devastating.

You can see the difficulty. Where the concept of rescission is allowed, the investor is placed in an absolutely no-lose situation. All he has to do is find a fund that is not registered in his state, then buy up all the shares he can afford. If the value of the shares goes up, that's fine. If they fall below what they originally cost him, that's great too. The investor merely has to scream, "Rescission!" He then enjoys a preferential refund price equal to his original purchase price, plus interest.

At the time of our rescission problem we were in a down market, and if the Texas people had prevailed, they would have received more money than their shares were then worth. They would have been placed in a favored position above our other investors, and that was a result we couldn't abide. So we said to Texas, "No dice!"

The Lone Star State met us head-on and went ahead with its action against us. We might have sustained their challenge, except for one thing: Our problem came to the attention of the SEC, and the federal bureaucrats, with their heavy legal artillery, lumbered into the act.

"My goodness," the feds said, "you have an *undisclosed contingent liability*." So they forced us to suspend sales and redemptions of the fund. Eventually, we were able to settle the dispute with the SEC, but at what cost! The biggest price we paid was that, as we moved through the slow court process, our fund couldn't accept any new sales. Finally, we were forced to wind up the business altogether. From a booming $20 million enterprise we went back to zero, thanks to the busybodies at state and federal levels. Our fund had been trapped by those Texans in a real old-fashioned financial "box canyon," from which there was no escape.

As my fund was losing this Texas shoot-out between 1971 and 1972, I hit bottom in my own personal bear market. Although I eventually extricated myself from any involvement with Investment Indicators, I emerged from the battle thoroughly bloodied. Because I had borrowed heavily for the company, my negative net worth—that's a polite term for how much you're in hock—was more than $100,000.

My personal life was in even worse shape. Largely because of the incredible strain I had been under, my marriage got into trouble. Soon, I found myself divorced.

Friends have asked me whether I ever thought of jumping off a building, as so many brokers did in New York during the Great Depression days. The answer is no, not once. All I thought about was straightening out my badly tangled affairs so that I could start all over again. I had made mistakes before, and I knew they should serve as stepping-stones to future successes rather than as signals of some ultimate, permanent defeat.

Granted, the debacle with Investment Indicators was worse than anything I had ever imagined, but I figured that since I had survived before, I could survive once again. In fact, the main thing I've learned about life in general, and investing in particular, is that it's absolutely essential to expect setbacks and to learn to overcome them. The ability to survive, to be resilient in even the worst of circumstances, is perhaps the foremost attribute of any successful investor, a fact that I began to understand at a young age.

My lessons in survival in all sorts of business situations began in the Sacramento Valley in California. I was born in Sacramento in 1937 and reared in a nearby small town named Woodland, where my father was the Yolo County district attorney. Although my father's life seemed to be interesting and rewarding, I was never interested in becoming a lawyer. From the very beginning I wanted to be an entrepreneur.

My first lessons in survival were quite basic: I learned early on that the only way you could make a go of any enterprise was, first, to find a profitable business concept; then begin to take practical steps to put the concept into action; and, finally, put in extra hours working to turn a profit. Now, all this may seem quite elementary. But it's amazing to me how many investors think they can make money just by coming up with a good idea, but without contributing the time, effort, and analysis to make their idea a reality.

I remember, as a boy, picking up walnuts, sacking them, and then selling them for $5 a 100-pound sack. (Those were the English walnuts, not the black ones that brought only $3.) There were some hard times and some tough investment decisions to be made, even in the nut business. Some other kids thought I was a little crazy, spending my free time rooting through the twigs and leaves.

Although plenty of people didn't want to buy, I quickly learned that if I kept at it and plowed right through the rejections, I would eventually get somebody to buy my wares. Moreover, if I wanted to accumulate extra spending money, I had to pick up *extra* walnuts. And if I wasted my effort on the cheaper but more plentiful $3 nuts, I'd earn that much less. One after another, these little lessons in capitalism began to accumulate in my young mind.

At about age twelve I moved up in the business world by launching a small chicken operation. I sold eggs from door to door, and continued the business even after we moved to Santa Barbara. By the time I was thirteen I owned a couple of dozen chickens.

My instincts for this business came naturally. As I learned many years later in graduate school, my little chicken farm was a *fully integrated operation* that took advantage of every aspect of chicken farming. I sold the eggs; I learned to kill and pluck fryers for market; and I developed a list of clients for my own chicken fertilizer.

As with the earlier, nut-gathering enterprise, I put in a lot of time to make the chicken business work. During the week I spent about an hour each morning or afternoon with the business, and two to three hours each day on the weekends. It took plenty of time to get the most mileage out of my fledgling investment. A couple of friends usually helped out, and I allowed them to share in the profits.

Of course, even with the hard work and extra help, sacrifices sometimes had to be made. Periodically, business wasn't so good, and one of my partners would get discouraged and drop out. But I already understood that you have to move through plenty of bad times if you hope to reach the good.

When I turned fourteen I liquidated the chicken business, including all the eggs, fryers, and fertilizer. This gave me a fairly decent profit and freed me for a more lucrative enterprise—caddying at the local golf course. In short, I had reached an age when conducting a chicken business, given the limited resources and space I had, couldn't match the potential income I could get on the links.

Because the chicken business had occupied me for several years, I had grown attached to the animals and to my customers. But at the same time I had learned that there was a time to hold and a time to sell. Adult investors today far too often stick with a stock, fund, or other investment that they know is bad, because they became too fond of a company. Or perhaps they just lack the get-up-and-go to unload it and buy something else.

This switch to a new enterprise provided more of a return than I had expected. The exposure to expert golfers helped me improve my own game, and I became the captain of my high school golf team. This achievement, in turn, helped open the door to Stanford University, a school that prides itself on excellence in that sport.

In college I learned several more important principles that were to stand me in good stead later in my own forays into investing:

- During the summers a variety of jobs requiring physical labor—including driving a tractor, cultivating sugar beets, toiling in an oil field, and serving as a switchman on two Chicago railroads—gave me insights into the grass roots operations of a number of different kinds of businesses.
- Buying and selling stocks through brokers while still an undergraduate helped me learn the "nuts and bolts" of the markets while risking only minimal amounts of cash.
- A stint as a life insurance salesman convinced me that permanent life insurance is a terrible investment.
- A few months of selling insulation door to door showed me I was particularly inept at personal sales.
- Working as a bank teller gave me a hands-on introduction to banking.

This self-education in investment and business opportunities, and also the discovery of personal strengths and weaknesses, are key phases in the making of a good investor. First, it's helpful to decide where your strengths and interests lie as an investor. Then, you concentrate your energies on the areas where you feel you're best qualified.

As for me, I liked the analysis of stocks and companies more than personal selling, so I gravitated toward investment research and analysis. The best advice came right after I graduated from

Stanford in 1959. The head man at Dean Witter research on the West Coast, told me, "Young man, if you want to enter this business and become a professional, the best thing for you to do is to go back to school and get your master's degree in business."

So off to Stanford Business School I went. But I didn't just rely on what I was learning at school, because I had already discovered that for an investor it's as important to get on-the-job training as to listen to instructors in a classroom. In fact, it's more important to get your hands dirty, get out into the marketplace, struggle a little, and make a few mistakes.

So I continued trading in the market while I was in graduate school, and I also began to work part-time for one Laverne Foster, who operated an investment advisory service. Laverne introduced me to many facets of the financial services business that I didn't know a thing about and that weren't taught in courses at business school.

We hit it off so well that I went to work for him as a full-time junior analyst after I graduated with my MBA in 1961. By age twenty-three I was a vice-president of Foster Investment Services and was gaining experience every day in publishing a small investment publication and managing individual portfolios. In my own estimation I was hot stuff. Very hot stuff.

In fact, I thought I was so good that in December 1962 I figured I could do better on my own. So two associates and I formed Mitchell, Morse & Schwab. Mitchell's name came first because he put up most of the money; Morse & Schwab did the "donkey work." The outlook for our venture was bright, with only the sky as the limit, or so we thought.

Right after the Cuban missile crisis we launched Investment Indicator, an investment advisory in the form of a semimonthly, eight-page newsletter. The first issue came out in January 1963.

Our features in the newsletter included an analysis of stock market cycles. We were predicting the beginning of a new "up" cycle. Our technique was to predict future movements of the market by evaluating a series of market indicators. The stock market is in many ways a "living organism," with a past history that contains the seeds of upcoming growths, "aging," and declines. At our high point we had some three thousand subscribers nationally, each of whom paid us $84 a year.

For the next eight to nine years we went through many struggles, but we learned how to survive in the investment business. Our newsletter was never very successful, but I developed a knowledge of what I now call "personal leverage" that has stood me in good stead in the ensuing years. I learned how to do things through people and services so that my own effectiveness and power in the investment field could be multiplied. This principle applies as easily to my own personal investing as it does to building an entire stock brokerage company.

For example, I learned to evaluate investment experts and rely heavily on those who offered the best advice. This period of experience also gave me invaluable insights into specialties like financing, marketing, merchandising, administration, and management—all key skills for evaluating the best companies in which to invest.

But even though the knowledge I was gaining about the investment business was great, the money I was making in those days wasn't. Within the first two years we ran out of money. I was on the brink of losing it all. Morse had already left, and I was drawing an almost nonexistent salary.

At that time we were only putting out the newsletter, which we believed was a good product, but we had no idea about how to merchandise it. We went through three or four different advertising agencies, but without success. It would have been easy to give up at this point. I had given it a good shot, and I was tired of crawling uphill, often hanging on only by my financial fingernails. But I decided to give it one more try. This time I hit pay dirt. I managed to locate a man named Jack Shelton, who introduced me to a new world—direct-mail marketing. We had been on the edge of the abyss, and without the genius of Shelton we would have been finished. But he and his firm turned us around, and all of a sudden our circulation picked up substantially.

Now things really began to move. Our firm established the Investment Indicators mutual fund, and I was sure that my fortune was made. But you already know what happened next: the great Texas rescission mess. So once more I was down, but still not quite out.

Even as I was being dogged by federal and state authorities in the early 1970s, I knew from past experience that I should stick to my guns. If I just refused to give up and tried to learn from the bad times, there was a better than even chance that somehow I'd eventually end up on top.

So I decided to execute a flank attack on the unruly investment business: Though at the nadir of my business and personal life, I established the First Commander Corporation, the forerunner of the present Charles Schwab & Co., with $100,000 borrowed from an entrepreneurial uncle, Bill Schwab.

However, my financial situation failed to improve immediately. In fact, to be honest, you might say things went from bad to worse. Months went by, with the rescission entanglement still not settled. By the end of 1971 my uncle became so disgusted that he sold his entire 100 percent of our company to me and four other officers. In a very decent gesture, he took only our notes in payment.

After we had struggled along for another year, my four fellow officers gave up. They sold out to me by turning over their stock in return for my assumption of their liabilities on the notes. So in 1973 I wound up owning 100 percent of the company—and being 100 percent in debt for everything.

But I had the company, and I believed in it. My first order of business was to get out from under my debts and get the banks paid off. Step by step, I put some deals together that got us out from under the terrible loan burden. For example, we received a $100,000 commission on a corporate financing deal, which involved arranging the sale of a lumber company to Louisiana Pacific. This enabled me to pay back a substantial portion of our company debts.

Meanwhile, my uncle, Bill Schwab, still had plenty of his old entrepreneurial fire left, and he also retained his faith in me. He had started his own money market fund prematurely, lost a bundle in it, and recouped his losses with a couple of outside investments. Then, in 1975, he decided to come back into Charles Schwab & Co.—there must have been something about the name that gave him confidence!

He agreed to acquire 30 percent of our corporation at the very time I needed to raise more capital. But he laid down one condition: At that time, we had one office in San Francisco, and he insisted that we open a branch in Sacramento, where he was then living. Also, he wanted to run this office himself.

"Come on, Bill," I said, "let's go to Los Angeles. That's where the big market is."

"No," he insisted, "I think there's a good market in Sacramento. Let's try here first."

He held the cards, that is, the capital that I needed, so I agreed, although I was sure that if we set up shop in Sacramento, only 100 miles away from San Francisco, we would find slim pickings, indeed.

To my surprise and delight, I was proved dead wrong. The Sacramento office took off. Our success there gave us the confidence not only for a move to Los Angeles, but also to many other communities throughout the country.

With this impetus we were off and running toward becoming a profitable enterprise. But one other event was necessary before we could really "hit a home run." I'm referring to the historic federal legislation that mandated that commissions on certain brokerage transactions could be negotiated. Furthermore, after a thirteen-month trial period under the legislation, commissions on *all* trades by stockbrokers became negotiable.

This final phase of the legislation, which is known as May Day in brokerage circles because it went into effect on May 1, 1975, became the bedrock of our later success as the nation's largest discount brokers.

True, there were still a number of obstacles to hurdle before we reached the peak, but we were well on our way. Following is a brief history of my growing company, which was the focal point of my personal investments as well:

At first, financing remained a continual struggle. Venture capitalists didn't find us venturesome enough. The Small Business Administration couldn't find our industry listed among approved borrowers. And we certainly weren't "bankable" by the major lending institutions.

When we turned profitable in 1976, the outlook began to change. American Asian Bank lent us $150,000. Later we managed to get $200,000 from what was then the Camino California Bank (the predecessor of the Imperial Bank) with a loan secured with my home. In fact, more than once when our firm was about to undertake a major commitment one of my associates would quip, "There goes Chuck's home on the line again."

Many banks, however, remained unimpressed. Crocker Bank severed a fourteen-year relationship with us. The Bank of America turned us down too—not once, but twice. We apparently didn't yet have a long enough track record to convince them we were a good risk.

In the spring of 1980, with the number of our clients and branches going up and our profits soaring, we decided to go public. But once again I ran across the old rule that failure stalks success. In short, the timing was simply premature to put the deal together.

Our plan had been to turn to our one hundred thousand customers at the time (today we have more than eight hundred thousand) by selling them shares. But the independent investment banking firms we had retained kept insisting on valuing the shares at less than we thought fair. Also, our registration statement disclosed our rapid growth, but also overemphasized our error accounts, which were temporarily high after we installed a new sophisticated computer system.

So we withdrew the public offering, to the delight of our full-commission competitors. They apparently forgot their own scandalous history of operational problems. But we were to have the last laugh—as the following demonstrates.

Tony Frank, chairman of United Financial Corporation, a subsidiary of National Steel, agreed to have United buy a 20 percent interest in our company. The deal was to give 1.5 million shares of Charles Schwab & Co. to United for $3.25 a share. That was a more than welcome infusion of capital for us and a highly profitable move for United, as well.

Finally, there came the crowning touch: Bank of America agreed to acquire our company for $53 million. There was no more crowing now from the full-commission fellows. It took about fourteen long months for the merger to wend its way through the Department of Justice, the Comptroller of the Currency, the SEC, and the Federal Reserve Board. At last, the U.S. Supreme Court affirmed the acquisition in June 1984.

The reason for all the careful scrutiny was that the federal officials had to be sure that the brokerage business was closely related to banking and that public benefits would clearly outweigh any adverse effects. But all, including the Fed, approved our merger with a bank in a landmark ruling.

These, then, are some of the milestones that marked our success, from the low point in the early 1970s to the apogee in the 1980s. There have been plenty of steep, downward dives along the way. And sometimes, the valleys seemed to continue so interminably that I myself have wondered whether there would be a recovery.

But this was all part of the learning process, all part of trying new approaches and acquiring new skills until everything came together in a final burst of success. For us in our discount brokerage business, there seem to be four "secrets," if you will, which have helped us to survive bad luck and serious setbacks, and to keep on the upward track.

First of all, since our inception we have relied on direct-response marketing. The emphasis is on dealing with individual investors, not on business with large institutions. We use a photograph of myself in our space ads to show that a human being runs this firm.

Secondly, we stress the cutting edge of computer technology. Many of our early mistakes came as a result of not being sufficiently efficient in our operations, but that is no longer true. Our advanced on-line computer system has made possible the twenty-second brokerage transaction, from putting in a buy or sell order to the final execution of that order. This technology has made us number one in the country in providing customer satisfaction, according to a Yankelovich poll of a dozen leading brokerage firms.

Thirdly, we constantly risk innovation. By introducing the twenty-four-hour, seven-days-a-week order entry service, we substituted "customer's hours" for the inconvenient broker's hours that are standard elsewhere. Also, we decided to offer a self-directed IRA account and Keogh plan, free of all fees. And we've begun to sell no-load mutual funds, an unheard-of move among brokerage houses.

Fourth, and most important, we have never acknowledged defeat, no matter how tough things became. It would have been easy to stop butting our heads against the seemingly impregnable wall of inadequate financing. But we tried every possible way to get through, around, or over that wall until we succeeded.

An instinct for survival—for rejecting rejection, for being resilient, and for solving problems that may appear insoluble at first—has been a key ingredient for me, both as an individual investor and as the founder of a brokerage business. I'm convinced that if you hope to succeed, this survival instinct must play a major role for you as well, as you embark on your adventure of becoming an independent investor.

3

What's a Stockbroker and Why Should You Trust Him?

WHEN you decide to put your money on the line by buying securities, the person who handles—or mishandles—your hard-earned cash is a stockbroker. But who exactly is this person, and what reason do you have to trust him or her?

To understand what a stockbroker is, it's necessary first to understand the environment in which he or she works. And that means the major stock exchanges. So let's begin with the most venerable and ossified of all those institutions, the New York Stock Exchange (NYSE).

The NYSE transacts 85 to 90 percent of the total volume of business in listed securities. Though technically a regional exchange, the NYSE is far and away the most important, as well as the largest, of all the equity exchanges in the country.

The Pacific, the Midwest, the Philadelphia and the Boston exchanges divide up the listed business that is left. But don't sell them short, they are a group of lively little Davids operating actively in the shadow of the sleepy Goliath of Wall Street, and they have successfully pioneered many major innovations in the way investments are handled. The rallying cry of the New York Stock Exchange might well be, "But we've always done it this way." The other exchanges, in contrast, are inclined to ask, "How can we do it better?"

If the controlling interest of the NYSE had its way, we would still be operating under fixed commission rates, and there would be no Charles Schwab & Co. as it exists today. So I'll readily admit my views on this exchange are somewhat biased. The other exchanges, on the other hand, took steps long ago to set up creative programs for the institutional investor, to facilitate the rebate of excessive commissions.

For innovation, the big brokerage firms take their cue from the NYSE. As I discussed in the previous chapter, negotiated rates for commissions were introduced generally in 1975. Brokers who wanted to take the discount route promptly dropped their rates by as much as 50 percent. At the same time, however, the major stock firms *increased* their rates by 7 percent!

I couldn't believe this when I heard about it back in the 1970s. When the law regulating rates was changed, I was sure that every brokerage house would lower rates in a rash of increased competition. But profits were the controlling motivation for many of the bigger firms. Displaying insensitivity toward the ordinary investor, they have since raised their rates again and again. So now they are some 20 to 25 percent above the original fixed commissions, and double what most discount brokers charge.

In these "full-service firms," as they call themselves—I call them "full-*commission* firms"—it's like extracting hen's teeth to get a simple schedule of their charges. If you doubt me, try it. Visit a Merrill or a Shearson/American Express office and find out for yourself. When investors talk, the brokers don't necessarily listen.

Whatever kind of brokerage firm is involved, there are two basic ways in which brokers place orders with the various exchanges. One is the auction method; the other is the electronic approach.

Broadly speaking, the NYSE still operates on the old auction system, while the regionals use both the auction and electronic methods. Technically, these are called *derivative* execution systems*—not an important term for your use, but you may hear an occasional broker refer to it. The Pacific Exchange uses the SCOREX electronic system; the Philadelphia, PACE; the Midwest, MAC. The names may vary, but the procedure is much the same.

Now, let's examine in detail how the auction approach and the electronic method work.

Suppose an institution wants to sell 5,000 shares of a $10 stock that is listed on the NYSE. The first step in the auction method is for the order to go down to the busy floor of the exchange to one of the brokerage representatives. This representative then approaches a *specialist* in that stock.

The specialist rides shotgun on a specified group of stocks, tracks the market in them all day long, and executes specific orders. Even if you own a seat on the exchange, that doesn't empower you to buy or sell without going through a specialist.

So the brokerage representative asks the specialist, "How's the market in XYZ stock?"

The specialist tells the broker what the going prices of the stock are, and the number of shares being offered. Then, the broker places an order at a certain price for 5,000 shares of stock on the books of the specialist, who holds it until he can match it with the incoming business or sells it from his own account.

When the customer places an order for a specific amount of stock at a definite price, it is called a *limited order*. But he or she might also choose to put in a *discretionary order*, which gives the floor representative some leeway to execute part of the order at a different price. In fact, there are a wide variety of possible orders: market orders to sell, market orders to buy, stop orders, not-held orders, and many more. But for our purposes it is enough just to know about the limit and market orders because these are the ones you're most likely to make.

As you can see, the auction approach to buying and selling may

---

*Derivative refers to prices based on the "primary market," i.e., the New York Stock Exchange.

take some time, several hours, in fact. You may even have to wait until the next day to find out about the final execution of your transaction.

But things are quite different with the modern, twenty-second method of electronic execution. The brokerage representative merely types the order into a computer and then presses a key that directs the order to the mainframe of the computer. The computer transmits the information directly into the exchange computer. Once the order is taken from the customer to the computer, no human hand touches the order. It travels at the speed of electricity to another electronic box sitting on the floor of the exchange, and there the transaction is consummated.

The client, waiting by the phone in the brokerage office, receives confirmation of his purchase in only about twenty seconds. About half of our Schwab orders are done in this manner. The rest—because of their large or oddball size (i.e., those not in multiples of 100)—are still completed under the old, slower auction format.

As for over-the-counter (OTC) stocks—or those not listed on a major exchange—the same ease and speed in executing orders is becoming the order of the day. New computer technology has enabled a few firms—and the number should grow rapidly—to complete an OTC transaction in about fifteen seconds.

Thanks to modern technology, before long you'll be transmitting many of your orders right through your Touch-Tone telephone or personal computer to your broker's computer without any human assistance. Still, all this talk about present wonders and wonders to come shouldn't obscure a basic human issue: It doesn't matter how quickly and efficiently the order is executed if it's a bum order. That unhappy possibility leads us right back to the doorstep of the broker you've chosen.

Is he competent? Is she free of conflicts of interest? Do you really *need* him or her?

The answer to each of these three questions is, all too often, a resounding NO! But it's not always the broker's fault. The reasons for his or her shortcomings are inherent in the very system that hires him.

When a traditional brokerage firm brings new stockbrokers on staff, the firm is primarily interested in his or her selling skills. If you've done a commendable job selling jewelry, automobiles, or photocopy machines, that will be counted as the first plus in the interviewing process. Your background in economics is not as important; neither is your expertise in understanding investments, nor your statistical ability. Just one skill is prized above all others: Can you sell?

I'm not exaggerating here. The brokerage firms make no bones about the qualifications for prospective brokers in their want ads. Just read a few of them, and you'll be forever wary when your own broker gives you his presumably disinterested, expert advice.

Of course, you are now probably thinking, "But surely in their training programs respectable firms make certain that their brokers become well grounded in all aspects of the business."

Oh, they learn the industry jargon, all right. For six months they read various manuals and master a basic knowledge of the field, things that any intelligent independent investor might master on his own. Then they take what's called the "Series 7" test. This is not an aptitude test, but just a general examination on the ABCs of the investment world.

Finally, they hold the lofty title of "Registered Representative" of their firm. That just means they have obtained a license through that firm to do business, and they are responsible to that firm. They also become registered with the stock exchanges with which the firm does business and in the various states where the firm has clients.

After his or her first six months to a year with a firm, the broker's compensation is mostly determined on a commission basis. It ranges from 30 to 50 percent of the commission you pay. Some firms call it "salary plus a year-end adjustment," but for the most part the bulk of what a broker earns is related to individual production. The unspoken guideline is, "Sure, advise the client, but, above all, *sell* him!"

Even for those going into management in a firm rather than working as on-line salespeople, the salary is usually based on the sales production of their unit. Also, the star sellers become wealthy and independent in their own right. And there's always the opportunity to skip to another firm if the offer is right. So the makeup of the personnel in a brokerage firm, their basic philosophy of work, and in fact the entire structure of the industry, comes down to that powerful, four-letter word: *sell!*

Now, it's not that I'm opposed to good, old-fashioned capitalism—good salesmanship has been a cornerstone of our economy, and I'm all for it—but there's salesmanship and then there's sales sleight-of-hand. What bothers me most about the full-commission brokerage firms is that, in my opinion, they sometimes go a step or two too far.

One of my main beefs is, as I've indicated earlier, that they enjoy higher commissions on higher-risk investments. The greater the risk to you as the buyer, the fatter the fee that goes to your broker. Such an inherent conflict of interest in a broker, who presumes to give you objective advice, would be enough to disgrace any holder of public office caught in a similar situation. But stockbrokers constantly escape with hardly a mild criticism.

Let me give you a typical case involving an oil and gas tax shelter, a high-risk venture for you and your money. Sure, if you lose your $10,000 investment, you'll get a 100 percent tax write-off, and there will be other significant tax deductions along the way. And if your exploration firm actually strikes oil, you'll not only get back your $10,000 but a huge profit as well. But the chances are that you won't strike oil, any more than you'll find a cache of buried pirate's treasure on your next trip to Florida. More likely, the money you put into this high-risk investment will disappear into a series of dry wildcat wells, and you'll end up with a tax shelter that contains nothing to be sheltered.

But what about your broker?

On this kind of deal he'll have to do a bit more work, hustle a little more, and hard-sell you a little harder. But don't weep for him. His firm's commission will be 8½ percent, or $850 (plus a few goodies when you read the fine print of the prospectus). Typically, the broker will get half of that, $425, or he may even re-

ceive 60 percent of the firm's commission. And if he sells an
unusually large amount to you, he may even get a free trip to the
Bahamas.

By contrast, let's say the broker recommended $10,000 worth
of a major company listed on the New York Stock Exchange, or
200 shares at $50 per share. In this case, for the firm the com-
mission would be $250, of which the broker would receive a mea-
sly 30 percent, or $75. Now, $425 or $75, which commission would
you choose? For that matter, which one would any sane person
choose? I don't blame the broker here so much as the screwball
system that fattens itself by increasing the risk to the client.

But with traditional stockbrokers there are problems other than
this high-risk, high-fee scenario. When you walk into Prudential-
Bache, say, or Dean Witter, it's "pot luck" what account executive you'll be dealing with. Chances are, though, that you'll be
shunted to the rookie of the day, the eager but inexperienced young
fellow just out of his training course. Thereafter, unless you change
firms, you'll be "married" to him, and he will slowly learn the brokerage business—at your expense.

Of course, some customers need to have their hands held. But
there are those who have an independent streak and want to try
out their wings to see if they can't do a better job than the average stockbroker. This is one of the reasons that the myriads of
discount brokers have popped up around the country, catering to
the entrepreneurial investor who wants to stand on his own two
feet and run his own show.

There are considerable differences in the way customers are
handled at the discount houses, as opposed to the full-commission firm. For example, here are some features that should char-
acterize a well-established discount broker:

- He'll charge you less, transaction for transaction, than a full-
  commission broker.
- He'll be a fully licensed stockbroker but be paid by salary, not
  by commission.
- He'll get extra compensation according to how well the company as a whole does, not how many individual sales he makes.

- She'll offer you an IRA account without charging you a commission other than the transaction commission on the stocks or whatever other investment is purchased for the account.
- She won't give you any "advice" or opinion about what kind of investment is best for you. It's even stated in our corporate commandments that we at Schwab won't do this, and if I find any violators of that policy, I'll fire them.
- She will provide information about the stock or other investment you want to buy, such as the nature of recent news reports on earnings per share as found in Dow Jones or Standard & Poor's publications.
- He will make it clear, if you should ask, that any investment decision is up to you.
- She may well be available to take your orders twenty-four hours a day, seven days a week.

So now you have a bird's-eye view, through my admittedly opinionated eye, of the stock exchange process and the brokerage system. Obviously, as a militantly enthusiastic discount broker, I have a point of reference. But I hope that through my own biases and sometimes iconoclastic beliefs some element of truth emerges that will fit your own approach to investments. I'm completely convinced that, unless you're a person who absolutely *must* have a shoulder to lean on when placing your investments, you'll be better off becoming your own stockbroker. You'll reap higher profits as you do your own analyses and make your own decisions. Furthermore, with your discount broker you'll place your orders for purchases more efficiently and at a much lower rate of commissions. You'll also have more fun!

But don't just take my word for it. Read on, and see if you feel you have what it takes to nudge your old stockbroker aside and step into the driver's seat. Our next topic, which gets right to the heart of the matter, focuses on some of the basic, practical principles that should guide you as you begin to put together your own personal investment portfolio.

4

Ten Basic "Secrets" of
Success in the Stock Market

To BE SUCCESSFUL in any activity it's necessary first to settle on a basic approach, a fundamental philosophy of action. Investing in the stock market is no exception to this rule. Before you even think about putting your money on the line, there are ten underlying principles, or "secrets," that you should know.

I put the word *secrets* in quotes knowing that these points are not secrets at all to the seasoned, successful investor. On the contrary, they are quite well known. But if you are new to the stock market game, you may be aware of only a few, if any, of them. And even if you consider yourself an old pro, it should be worthwhile rethinking these fundamentals and making sure they are a practical part of your present investment strategy.

Secret 1: The stock market is moved primarily by emotion.

The mass psychology that guides the market is the biggest single factor you must understand if you hope to become a successful investor. This emotional and psychological ingredient often has absolutely nothing to do with the state of the economy, but it exerts an overwhelming power on the movement of the market.

Rumors are prime movers of the stock market. Take a recent situation involving a reported stand taken by President Ronald Reagan. Just a few days before he announced he would stand for reelection, a story swept the financial community that he would not run again, possibly because his wife, Nancy, was ill.

The result? On this unsubstantiated rumor the Dow Jones Industrial Average, which had risen 7 points earlier in the day, closed down 10.99 points. Some thought the rumor had started in the Midwest or on the West Coast. Others believed it had come out of Canada. One person even said he had heard it from his cousin on the floor of the New York Stock Exchange. A caller to Mrs. Reagan's press secretary said he'd heard that Henry Kissinger was repeating the story.

A closely related perennial rumor influencing the market, which crops up about every six months, says the president has suffered a heart attack. Inevitably, Nervous Nellies rush to dump their holdings, often precipitating a general market decline. Of course, the president always turns up in the best of health, but that's not the point. The point is the power of psychology on the movement of the markets. The stock market usually "anticipates" the movement of the national economy by six to nine months; in effect, the "mood" of the market lets us know in advance what we can expect with regard to our business health, inflation rate, and other concrete economic factors.

There's nothing new of course about this emotional factor. Throughout history there have been fads and fashions in investing that had lives of their own. For example, there was the "tulip mania" in Holland more than two hundred years ago, when Dutch investors went crazy over the prospect of making huge sums of money on their flower bulbs.

More recently you may remember when, in the 1960s, recreation-related stocks were the "in" thing. The people who made the bowling alleys and bowling balls were the darlings of the market. Every man, woman, and child, it seemed, was going to have a personal bowling alley. But within about a year and a half, some bowling alley people who had gone public went broke.

So if you hope to make money in the market, it's absolutely essential that you begin to understand the importance of psychology. As a general rule on emotions, let me say this: If you respond to each fad and rumor, you're sure to end up a loser, but if you learn to discern the *broader* movements in the market, in contrast to those produced by a series of short-term emotional factors, you're more likely to do better.

That brings me to my second "secret"—how to begin to perceive and use the great cycles of the market.

Secret 2: The market moves in long, identifiable cycles of bull and bear activity.

You can never be a successful investor until you correctly judge "which end is up"—that is, whether you're generally in the up or down phase of a long cycle of market activity. You have to ask yourself one major question before you pull out your checkbook: "At this point in time, do I think the market is headed up for a while, or is it likely to head down?" Or, to put it in brokerish lingo, "Am I in a bull or a bear market?"

But there's an important corollary to this principle that you might file away in your head as a warning. Some people think they have the ability to spot the top of a bull market or the bottom of a bear phase. Don't fall into this trap! Believe me, *nobody* can do this infallibly. It's impossible. The key is just to perceive in general when you're in an up or a down market, and then buy or sell your securities accordingly.

Another corollary is: Since you can't know precisely the low or high point in a cycle, it's best to have at least half of your investment capital always in equities (or common stock).* That way, if you're wrong and find you're in an ongoing upward trend, you won't lose out entirely. So I would recommend that you stay 50

---

*Equities are securities that represent partial ownership in a company. I use the terms *equities*, *common stock*, and *equity stock* roughly synonymously. Also, equity funds are the same as common stock funds.

percent invested in equity stocks during what you consider to be a bear, or down, market, and 100 percent invested during what you perceive as a bull, or up, market.

Now, let's go into the mystery of the market cycles in a little more detail. The tricky thing is that these cycles usually *precede* the economic cycles. The highly emotional market "anticipates" well in advance the upward and downward swings in the economy. For instance, stocks go up in expectation of rising profits, but down in anticipation of declining profits.

Of course, there are many facets to our economy, countless political, social, and business elements that go into an upward or downward trend in the overall financial health of the nation. So if you plan to get into the market, I'd suggest that you study a detailed and reliable chart that compares key historical events with the movement of a major stock barometer, like the Dow Jones Industrial Average or the Standard & Poor's 500 composite. Then you'll begin to get a feel for how a war, an economic recession, or a presidential election may influence the market cycle.

One chart like this, which I have hanging on the wall of our boardroom, was created by X. W. Loeffler of Westwood, New Jersey. It lists every major economic and political event between 1920 and 1975, and ties them in with the movements in the Dow Jones Industrial Average. Apparently Mr. Loeffler did not bring the chart entirely up to date. This Dow Jones graph gives the stock values over the years of the thirty Dow Jones companies that comprise more than 20 percent of the value of the total market price of all the securities listed on the New York Stock Exchange.

By studying such a chart you can discover what I learned the painful way about stock market cycles back in 1962. (We've included a similar one showing the history of the Standard & Poor's index on the following pages.) It was then that I found out a crash in the market can be precipitated by events that are mostly psychological, not economic. Actually, the economy had just a simple dimple in its performance that year. The strong performance and outlook for the nation's business caused me to load up on equity stock. But that year President Kennedy went after U.S. Steel, and the Cuban missile crisis occurred. Investors thought that the

Stock Market History Since 1926

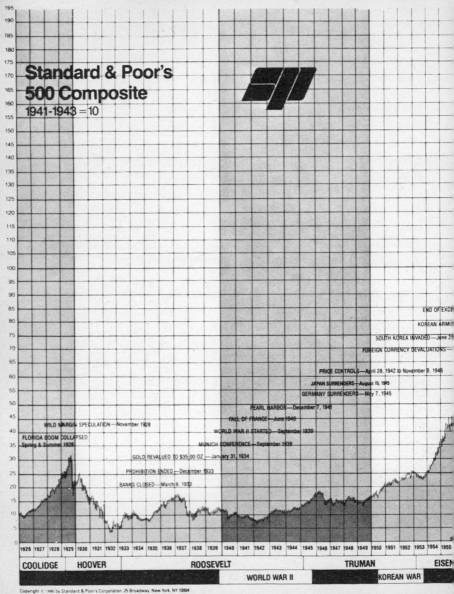

Standard & Poor's
500 Composite
1941-1943 = 10

END OF EXCE
KOREAN ARMIS
SOUTH KOREA INVADED—June 2
FOREIGN CURRENCY DEVALUATIONS—
PRICE CONTROLS—April 28, 1942 to November 9, 1946
JAPAN SURRENDERS—August 15, 1945
GERMANY SURRENDERS—May 7, 1945
PEARL HARBOR—December 7, 1941
FALL OF FRANCE—June 1940
WILD MARGIN SPECULATION—November 1928
WORLD WAR II STARTED—September 1939
FLORIDA BOOM COLLAPSED
MUNICH CONFERENCE—September 1938
Spring & Summer 1926
GOLD REVALUED TO $35.00 OZ.—January 31, 1934
PROHIBITION ENDED—December 1933
BANKS CLOSED—March 6, 1933

| 1926 | 1927 | 1928 | 1929 | 1930 | 1931 | 1932 | 1933 | 1934 | 1935 | 1936 | 1937 | 1938 | 1939 | 1940 | 1941 | 1942 | 1943 | 1944 | 1945 | 1946 | 1947 | 1948 | 1949 | 1950 | 1951 | 1952 | 1953 | 1954 | 1955 |

| COOLIDGE | HOOVER | ROOSEVELT | TRUMAN | EISEN |

WORLD WAR II   KOREAN WAR

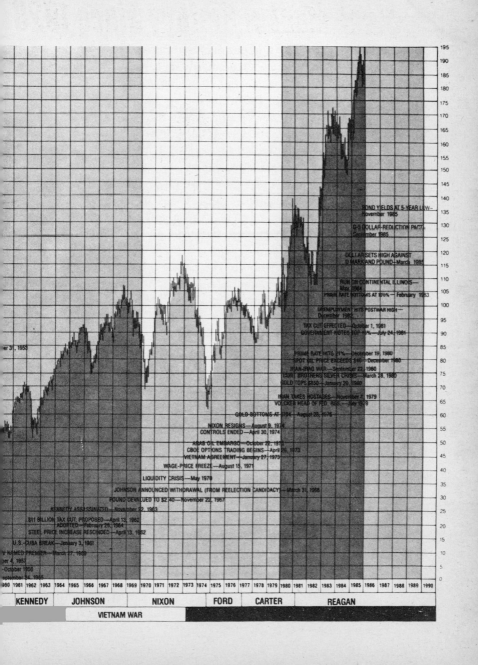

end of the world was upon us. In fact, you hear it almost as much at certain times in investor circles as you see it chalked on railroad underpasses: "The end is near!"

Of course, the end wasn't near. But because so. many people *thought* it was, the market went down, and a lot of people lost money, including myself. But after you spend a little time seeing how often the market goes up and down, and the circumstances surrounding its movements, you get a little wiser.

Take yourself. Let me hazard a guess. If you happen to be in the market already, you first got your feet wet near the end of an up cycle, right? That's when people are talking up the stock market—and when it's one of the worst times to invest! When the market's up and everyone is bragging about his or her success story, there's a dangerous euphoria in the air. It is easy to fall into this trap.

A seasoned investor who has developed a stout heart over the years will buy when the timorous sell. That's typically the time when everyone else moans and groans and talks about switching into gold or real estate. More often than not, many sell their equities at big losses. That's the time for you to think seriously about buying.

Although nobody can consistently guess the lowest point of the market, if you buy at a point anywhere near the nadir, when fear grips most investors, you'll profit in the long run. The important thing is to get a solid sense of the cycles so that you avoid investing every dime you own near the top of the market.

Learning about these broad market cycles can give you both courage and confidence. It's reassuring, when all around you are talking gloom and doom, to know approximately where you are in a cycle. Most investors either are not broad-cycle-oriented, or they're looking for the quick killing. You, though, are in it for the long haul, and you can afford to bide your time, over months or even years if necessary, until the cycle seems right for you to commit your hard-earned money.

For example, in the spring of 1982 I showed that I had learned this lesson about the cycles fairly well, a lesson I didn't understand back in 1962, when I was twenty-five years old. In the spring of 1982 my study of cycles made it clear to me that we were near a low point. It was a simple deduction because the Dow Jones Industrials had sunk to a level hundreds of points below its high just a few years before. I deduced this from the Dow Jones charts available in any library.

Another of the clear signals that caught my attention and made me realize that it was time to buy was that everyone was once again talking about the end of the world, the massive international crisis, and this bogeyman and that catastrophe. It seemed obvious to me that the time was nearing for a market recovery. So I bought shares in several growth-oriented mutual funds. I was fairly sure these funds would respond like the general upward movement I expected in the overall stock market.

We didn't hit the bottom until a few months later, in the summer of 1982. But the market did bottom out then, and it soon headed up like a rocket, and so, by the way, did my mutual funds.

Before we leave this subject of market cycles, let me make one more important point. The general direction of the stock market in the United States has always been up. So even if you find at first that you can't quite grasp how the cycles work, there's a way to take advantage of this upward movement, namely, a simple method of investing called *dollar cost averaging*.

This method involves investing an equal amount of money at regular intervals—say, monthly—in a diversified group of stocks. If your funds are limited, the best vehicle for this is a growth-oriented, common-stock mutual fund. I've already mentioned these funds briefly, and we'll get into them in more depth in a later chapter. But the key principle to keep in mind here is to pick a fund with a good growth record and then to put in regular amounts at the same time each month. This way you'll take advantage of the *general* upward movement of the market, even if you aren't able to bunch the purchase of your investments at the low end of a market cycle and your sales at the high end.

Secret 3: Diversify your investments.

This is just a fancy way of saying don't put all your eggs in one basket. Many times an inexperienced, unwary investor will read about a hot "field of the future" and then will get a tip about some stock that is supposed to be the next IBM of that field.

Look at oil and gas! Only yesterday, it seems, we thought we would all be living by candlelight again because of the shortages. Oil prices rose. Then we deregulated to a great degree. New supplies became available, and now we don't even talk about shortages. Those who plunged all their funds into oil and gas securities, thinking they had found the end-all bonanza, are not happy, to put it mildly. It may be that, over the long haul, oil and gas will be good vehicles for your money; so may computer companies and other electronic firms. But when enthusiasm becomes euphoria, beware!

Genetic engineering is one of the most recent illustrations that comes to mind. All the major firms in this area went public, but then later dropped from their high values by 50 to as much as 80 percent. Again, they may represent a great long-term investment, a good item to include with many other items in a broad-based personal portfolio, but they're not the thing to hold exclusively.

So all your investment eggs shouldn't be in any one basket, or you may find your basket has suddenly become quite empty.

Secret 4: Don't worry about a company's debt.

If a company you're considering investing in has enjoyed a high rate of return on capital for a consistent period, don't worry about its level of debt. Certain broker-salesmen may rattle off information about debt analyses, leasehold improvements, and other minutiae, but, frankly, it's a waste of time.

I've spent a lot of my lifetime in securities analysis, and I've found that you can all too easily bury yourself in nonessentials. Some of the pros may be able to make sense out of a company's debt picture, but you should forget it and concentrate on other issues.

Secret 5: Do a quick check of revenue per employee.

This may sound complicated, but it's not. Moreover, this calculation can show you a great deal about the attractiveness of a company as an investment in comparison with its competitors.

The idea is to determine how many dollars of revenue the firm makes per worker. This figure will provide a rough reflection of a company's productivity level, and that's important. After all, with more efficiency comes greater financial health. For one thing, the company that has the extra money can afford to do more research and development. High productivity also allows a company to experiment with more innovative techniques, to reinvest in itself, and to be in a better position to pay dividends, a key consideration for the individual investor.

You can easily find in the annual report the figures you need to make this revenue-per-worker calculation. If, for example, the company had $150 million in total revenues and 2,000 employees, the revenue per worker would be $75,000. When you see productivity declining over a series of annual reports, then something negative is probably happening within the organization. When the opposite is going on, the picture for the investor is much rosier. Finally, when comparing companies in the same industry, I would often go with the one with the higher revenue per employee because that one probably has the better management.

Secret 6: The price/earnings ratio is a red herring.

The ratio of a company's stock price to the company's earnings per share merely reflects, in a general sense, the attitude of the investing public toward a company. As a result, it is psychologically based and fluctuates all over the map. Some investors are drawn irresistibly to companies with low price/earnings (P/E) ratios because they feel the companies are undervalued. But that is certainly not always the case. The P/E ratio is definitely no magic formula for success with a stock, and it may well lead you 180° in the wrong direction.

I don't believe you can assume that a company with a stock

price of ten times its earnings per share is a better investment than one with a 20/1 ratio, nor do I think the latter stock would necessarily be a bad investment. If a company has maintained a high growth rate and it's in the up cycle of the market, you will make a lot of money even if you pay 20 times its earnings per share for it.

Secret 7: Stay flexible.

For a while, the great investment guru Joseph Granville was magic. He would go on stage and do his song-and-dance predictions in vaudeville fashion. He was famous for foreseeing the bear markets, but then he missed the greatest bull market of our lifetime in 1982–83.

Why did Granville fall flat on his face? Because he remained frozen to a position. He just couldn't unbend and become flexible, an absolute *must* for every independent investor. When you become "religious" in your market convictions, you lose your balance—the stock exchanges and your broker's offices are definitely not houses of worship.

In my own career as an investment adviser, I have observed classic cases of stubbornness and a total lack of flexibility. A wealthy individual began selling Xerox short—that is, he was betting that the stock would plunge. But, from 1963 to 1965, Xerox doubled, tripled, and quadrupled, and he still kept selling it short!

When you sell short, you've pledged to deliver a stock at a stipulated price before you've actually purchased the stock. To deliver it, you then have to buy it at the going market price, which may have risen from $10 (where perhaps it was when you started your speculation) to $100.

Xerox continued to sell more and more photocopiers, but the stubborn investor, certain he would eventually be proven right, kept losing more and more of his money. Finally, he had to liquidate his position, and his fortune was wiped out.

In my book, he violated just about every cardinal rule of investment: He failed to reckon on the long-term growth of the economy; he failed to diversify; and he failed to remain flexible.

Also, and this gets us into our next secret, he speculated by selling short, a strategy you should *absolutely* stay away from.

Secret 8: Spurn the temptation to speculate.

I'm not talking here about the fun-filled, exciting, and harmless practice of risking a small percentage of your assets—say, about 5 percent—on volatile or long-shot investments. You stand to lose little with this type of speculation and, who knows, you might even make a bundle.

No, here I'm referring to big-time speculation, involving huge chunks of your capital. The guy in the previous anecdote, who lost all his money by speculating to sell Xerox short, is a good example. When you own a stock outright, the worst, the very worst, thing that could possibly happen is that the stock might go to zero.

But when you sell short, you could lose all your money. This door to investment is marked *DISASTER* in capital letters. In fact, it's not investment at all; it's insanity.

Secret 9: Be bearish on bonds.

The conservative but naive investor may think it's safest first to go into bonds and then to try his luck with stocks. Sometimes this person may even think he can get 100 percent protection from the ups and downs of the market. What he doesn't understand is that bonds, beautifully printed on official-looking paper, as most of them are, can ping-pong about in value just like stocks. They may be especially volatile in times of inflation and changing interest rates.

For example, let's take a twenty-year, $10,000 bond paying 10 percent interest, usually in the form of a $500 check every six months. Now, suddenly, general interest rates go up to 15 percent. In that case, if you have to sell the bond, you'll get far less than its $10,000 face value—that is, $6,666, or a loss of one-third of your principal. Why? Because to match the general interest rate, the price of the bond must fall so that its yield at maturity will rise to the going 15 percent rate.

Of course, if you hold it to its twentieth-year maturity date, the bond will pay the $10,000 face value. But in the meantime you'll be getting far less than the going rate of interest. And if you do have to unload it early, you'll lose much of your capital investment.

Still, there is a bright side to this picture. Suppose the general interest rates skid to an average of 5 percent, or only half the rate you're enjoying from the bond. This would increase the security's value to $20,000. This is another example of the basic rule that as interest rates rise, bond prices fall; but, on the other hand, as interest rates drop, bond prices climb.

Unfortunately, I believe the outlook in general over the next few decades is for higher rather than lower interest rates and inflation, meaning that the outlook for bonds isn't too great. My advice is to make them only a small part of your portfolio, if you buy them at all. And if you do purchase any, it's a good idea to do it through a diversified bond mutual fund, to reduce your risk.

Secret 10: Rely on at least two solid, independent sources for investment advice.

I pick two sources here so that you'll always have access to a second opinion. In case there's a tie about whether you should buy, sell, or wait, you'll have to step in yourself to serve as a tie breaker. Under no circumstances should you rely on just one adviser, and especially not only one stockbroker.

There's a story I can tell about myself to illustrate this point. In the early 1960s, shortly after I graduated from business school with an MBA, I embarked on a career as a full-time professional securities analyst. Although I lost a lot of money and suffered blow after blow to my ego during the downturn of 1962, I still had a measure of cockiness left. So when some close friends of my parents sought my advice, I pontificated.

They were an elderly couple who had come over from Austria many years before. Also, they had put their life savings into various investments, one of which, at that time, looked like a real loser. It was Chrysler . . . twenty-two years ago!

The stock had hit a new low in 1962, and the company seemed about ready for bankruptcy. The couple had already suffered their loss because the stock seemed to have hit bottom, but I advised them on the basis of Chrysler's past history to sell anyhow. I only hope that they did not.

You see, a genius named Lynn Townsend emerged as leader of the company and turned Chrysler around, just as Lee Iacocca did twenty years later. In fact, the entire auto industry turned itself around. In the next three years the stock soared 400 to 500 percent. To this day I don't know whether the couple followed my advice, and thereby missed making a killing. But for me this was a humbling experience because it showed me how shaky most stock investment advice is and what a chance you take if you rely on just one "expert" to help you make your decisions.

But that brings me to the main question: Where should you go to find your two trustworthy advisers?

Not to brokers, certainly. You'll find that in brokerage research there are about one hundred buy recommendations for every one recommending a sale. It's "buy, buy, buy" all the time—even at the wrong time. Then, when the inevitable bear market hits, it's Depression City at home in the evening and Panicville during the workday.

Instead of a brokerage house, I suggest first that you subscribe to an advisory service that may track stock market cycles, growth companies, mutual funds, or various other areas of investment. You can get many of these services, such as the Value Line Investment Survey or Standard & Poor's Outlook, at your local library.

You should also spend some time each day reading *Barron's, The Wall Street Journal, Money* magazine, *Forbes,* or one of the other established investment publications. The more you read in the investment area, the better your judgment will be when you're faced with an investment choice.

As far as personal advice is concerned, talk to friends in some of the companies and industries that interest you. If you don't have any friends there, make them. You don't need to know the president of the company, either. I've found company shipping clerks can often give me a good reading on the state of a business's health if I just ask, "How's business?"

You might also seek out those acquaintances who are also interested in investments, and then arrange to meet regularly and bounce ideas off one another. Some very successful investment clubs have gotten their start this way.

The guiding principle behind seeking advice, however, is to make sure it's solid. Don't go off half-cocked following the latest tip, rumor, or "insider" leak. Perhaps the best description that I've heard of this kind of questionable advice goes like this: "They're not the bulls or the bears—they're the bum steers!"

It may be that many of these ten "secrets" for success in playing the stock market weren't secrets to you at all. They are principles that have been around for quite a while, and if you've done any investing at all, you've probably heard of at least some of them. But I think they provide us with a good, practical foundation for our next step in the investment adventure. Let's now take a close look at the specific key indicators in the economy that can help you spot the ups and downs of the highly emotional stock market.

5

How to Spot the Ups and Downs of the Market

SOME TIME AGO, a retired milkman won a nationwide investing contest. "What are your principles of investing?" he was asked.

"The one thing I've learned is to ignore everything economists say," he replied.

I couldn't agree more.

If you want success in the stock market, you must take the opinion of any economist with a grain of salt. And if you hear a consensus opinion by a gaggle of them, that's the worst piece of information you can get. It's almost certain they are wrong. The problem is that they are always busy measuring what happened yesterday and before yesterday, but they seem constitutionally incapable of predicting accurately what will happen tomorrow. Even worse, modern economics has little relationship to the whys and wherefores of the stock market.

The zany thing about all this is that these economists always get a wonderful press. In particular, their most *depressing* forecasts become coveted copy for most of the major newspapers. Then, when the "experts" finally start getting aggressive and optimistic about the economy, it has usually moved far ahead of them.

But if you ignore the economists, to whom or what should you listen?

Ultimately, the only safe source on which to rely is yourself. Of course, you have to make an effort to develop a kind of internal checklist to gauge the movements of the markets. But if you do a little homework, you can begin to cultivate your own personal barometer for proper investing. If you stick with it, you'll eventually find you have acquired a set of almost instinctive reactions that will often signal the presence of a bear or bull phase in the market cycle.

One of the best ways I know to develop this sense of the ups and downs of the market is to study, understand, and watch over a period of months several "investment indicators" that relate to market movements. There are ten of these indicators that I myself use. They've become such an automatic part of my approach to investing that often I don't realize I've relied on them until my investment decision has already been made. You can find these figures and concepts in publications put out by the Dow Jones Company, such as *Barron's* and *The Wall Street Journal*. Also, the Value Line Investment Survey computes many of these trend lines, and you'll find others in *Forbes, Business Week,* and other periodicals.

Following are the ten indicators, with a brief explanation of each. These indicators, by the way, are meant to be considered together. If you rely on only one or two in making your investment decisions, that will be like trying to fly a plane with one instrument. Only the entire package gives you a sense of the overall movement of the market.

Indicator 1: Become familiar with the general market movements and where you stand in the current cycles.

The first step is to get a market cycle chart that goes back at least five to ten years, so that you have an idea of how the major averages have moved. You might get the Dow Jones Industrials, the Standard & Poor's 500, the Value Line Index, or any others that would show the overall sweep of the market. Then you'll have a better picture in your own mind of where you stand in light of the ups and downs of the past few years.

When I first entered the stock market, I didn't have any idea of where we were in the movement of the general market. As a result, I unknowingly got caught in a downward cycle, and I lost a lot of money. (I'm assuming, by the way, that the overall movement of the market will be up. If you can't accept this assumption, you should exchange this book for one of the Bibles of Doom that are always available to more negatively oriented investors.)

Indicator 2: Look at the relationship between the net free reserves of the banking system and interest rate levels.

If the interest rates are quite high and they have made their major move upward in recent months, you know that the Federal Reserve System is probably trying to control credit more. Eventually, the "Fed" will win and send the business cycle into a recessionary period. Couple this with the fact that the "Fed" is probably making banks tighten up on credit and causing the net free reserves of the banking system to move downward and you have signs of negative pressure on the economy. The net free reserves figure is a special calculation you can find each Friday in *The Wall Street Journal* and also in graphs put out by the Federal Reserve Bank of St. Louis.

All these signals, taken together, should tell you that the government's policy is to cool down the business cycle. Since the stock market cools long before the economy does, you can expect your equity shares to start moving downward shortly, if they haven't declined already. The time has probably arrived to sell or hold, but not to buy.

Indicator 3: Watch the new high/low list on the New York Stock Exchange.

When you see a large number of new lows being recorded from day to day or week to week—say, in excess of a thousand per day—

you are probably in a low area of the market; certainly, you're not in a high phase. The market is saying it's in a state that is the opposite of euphoric, and the time is approaching to buy.

On the other hand, when the number of new highs for the year starts by far to exceed the new lows, and volume in general begins to reach new peaks, that's a sign you're well along in a rally. So that may be the time to sell or hold and certainly eliminate any stock margin.

Indicator 4: Look at the trends in price-earnings ratios.

You'll recall that in the previous chapter I told you to ignore P/E ratios, but that was in reference to the ratios of individual stocks. On the other hand, when you group many stocks together, the P/E figures become more meaningful. *The Wall Street Journal* carries these figures, but I use the fifty-stock index in *Barron's* magazine.

When the overall P/E ratios start to get low, where you're in the area of five to eight times earnings, you are most likely in the lower cycle of the market. That's the time to think about buying. But when they rise to ten to fourteen, or twelve to fifteen, you're definitely not at the beginning of a new bull market; you're at least midway or even further along in an upward phase. Selling or holding—but certainly not adding to—your shares may be more in order at this point.

Indicator 5: Watch market volume.

High volume on the New York Stock Exchange usually means the market is up and frenzied. Low volume means there is a negative, bearish feeling. What is "low" or "high" is relative, depending on where you are in the market's overall history. Although 50 million shares traded in a day may have been a high volume a decade ago, that may be a rather low volume today.

Indicator 6: Check the "overbought" and "oversold" indicators.

This is a calculation based on stocks advancing on a given day and on those declining. Where the stock market has been overbought, an excessive number of issues have advanced; where it's been oversold, an excessive number of issues have been unloaded by investors. Various financial publications run ongoing averages of this indicator. For example, you can find these figures in Value Line and in Standard and Poor's Trendlines.

If the market is in an overbought condition, that's a sign that investor euphoria has taken over, so the time may have arrived for you to stop buying, and perhaps even to sell. If the market is oversold and the market cycle seems to have declined to a relatively low point, you may want to consider increasing your buying.

Indicator 7: New issue offerings can be a reliable market barometer.

If you read that the new issues market—those stocks just then being offered to the public—is really hopping, you know you are moving into a frenzied, speculative phase of the market. Probably, you're close to a short-term top-of-a-market cycle, and so it's time to consider selling or holding on to your present position. In any case, don't add to your position.

Indicator 8: Look at some of the speculative indexes.

There are a number of these around these days, including indexes that track high-tech companies. In the past I've used the Barron's 20 Low Price Stock Index. Usually, if you're two-thirds of the way along in a bull market, the speculative stocks are moving much more quickly than they do normally. Then, as the market advances still further, you begin to see the average dividend yields on the market indexes of these stocks dropping and their combined P/E ratios climbing.

Indicator 9: Study prime interest rates.

It's certainly helpful for the growth of the economy and of the market these days if the prime rate is under 9 percent. That's quite low compared with its levels just a few years ago around 20 percent. Of course, some people will object, "The prime rate in 1953 was 2.5 percent! We won't have a good market until it gets down there again!"

That's baloney. The significance of the prime rate is relative and depends on where it has been in *recent* years.

Generally speaking, when interest rates are stable or declining, that's good for the stock market. When they are rising, that's bad for the stock market. The general rule is that rising interest rates will lead to moderating economic conditions and will increase the costs of doing business.

Indicator 10: Check leading business indicators.

These indicators, reported once a month in *The Wall Street Journal,* include such items as business inventories, new housing starts, and retail store sales, and they can be found in most of the leading business periodicals. They are also reported every month by the federal government. Although these are not early indicators for the movements of the stock market, they do confirm that the economy is in the process of moving in one direction or another.

Usually, the leading indicators move up just behind the market, some three to five months after a bull market has started. While they lead the business and economic cycles, they lag behind the cycle of the stock market.

Be especially alert when the business indicators begin to lose some of their momentum and perhaps start to stay stable, rather than go up. When this happens, there's a good chance you're at an "older" part of the bull market, or the final phases of upward movement. At this stage, the market has become vulnerable to significant declines just because of the natural movement of market cycles.

What should you do when you see such a signal? Become more

cautious in your buying. Do *not* move aggressively into speculative stocks. But I wouldn't go overboard: I don't believe in cashing out of a market completely. You should always remain invested. Remember, one of the "secrets" listed in the last chapter suggested that you should always keep at least 50 percent of your assets in the market. This way you don't lose out on an unexpected upward movement if you happened to have guessed wrong.

Along with these ten indicators, there are many other factors that you may want to add to your system as you make your investment decisions. For example, in low periods of the economy, you'll typically see more bankruptcies and other problems in the nation's business. Also, at various times in the past, factors like the odd-lot short sales by small investors have been regarded as good indicators.

But behind all these factors is the ingredient of mass emotion. So I want to emphasize once more that you have to become a market psychologist as much as a market analyst. Sometimes, the best signal for you to act is when you find yourself throwing down your financial newspaper in total disgust and asking, "Will the sky ever turn blue again?"

Or you may be playing golf or tennis with a friend, and you'll hear him say, "Ugh! The stock market is just awful, isn't it? It's all so depressing!"

Those are the times to think about becoming more aggressive in your buying!

On the other hand, there are times when you're feeling especially exuberant about the performance of your investments. Or you see increasing numbers of your friends on the phone with their brokers, buying everything in sight. At those moments it's best to back off, get control of your own emotions, and think about selling some of your holdings.

As you let these indicators merge into your understanding of the overall psychology of the market, you'll find that the process of developing good market judgment and sensitivity doesn't occur overnight. It takes time, usually years for the best investors. For a while you have to assume you're going to see the trees instead of the forest. But if you look at these indicators at least once a week and occasionally play with them in your mind, you'll soon find you're getting the *feel* of how they work. Your facility with these figures and concepts will grow substantially as you put more of your own money into various stocks and securities and begin to see up close exactly how they move.

Then, suddenly, large chunks of investment wisdom will begin to fall into place in your mind. So when that friend on the tennis court starts talking about how depressing the market is, a light will go on in your head. You'll say to yourself, "Hmmm. Interesting. People are starting to talk negatively about the market."

Then the front page of your local paper will report, "Stock Market Hits New Low." And you'll think, "I know there's an awful psychological mood afoot. I *should* feel depressed. But this just might be the time I should get some money together and start investing aggressively."

That's the point when abstract indicators begin to take on practical significance. They can help you evaluate the emotional mood. Then, if the indicators and the emotions of the market seem right for a purchase, you'll inevitably find yourself asking, "Exactly *what* should I buy?" The answer to that question may well depend on your present age and family situation, and on where you find yourself in your personal "life cycle," our next topic for discussion.

6

Life-Cycle Investing

WHERE are you in your life cycle? The answer to this question has far-reaching implications for your approach to investing. The needs of an investor younger than thirty-five are strikingly different from those of someone between thirty-five and fifty-five. Moreover, the investment style of a person who is fifty-five or older diverges considerably from the objectives of younger people. And the age of your children, if you have any, at any phase of your life cycle injects still another variable into the investment equation.

Our goal in this chapter is to provide a few guidelines about how to invest during different periods of your life. But let me say at the outset of this discussion that I realize it's impossible to lay down hard-and-fast rules that will apply to everyone in each age group. These suggestions are meant as guidelines, and only guidelines—not inflexible fiats from the Great Broker in the sky.

First of all, no matter what your age or family situation, there are certain preliminary, investment-related matters that everyone should consider making part of a complete portfolio. These include:

The fallback fund. I always recommend that you keep at least a couple of months' salary, perhaps even as much as six months', in some highly liquid form, such as a bank's high-interest account or money market fund. This will cushion you against the unknown and unforeseeable: poor health, accident, loss of your job, or other family crisis.

Life insurance. This is the best hedge against that ultimate family crisis, the death of a breadwinner or the primary child-care person. Inexpensive term life insurance will protect your family against premature death. Every conscientious parent and spouse has to consider this option.

If you're single and have no one dependent on you, all you need is burial insurance and enough to pay off your debts. That way, you leave this world even-Stephen.

If you're married or divorced and supporting children, figure out the monthly living expenses of those dependents. A nonworking spouse and family of two will probably need at least $2,000 or $3,000 a month to live on, and you should give them at least three to five years of protection at that rate. Then, there are child-care expenses if the surviving spouse plans to work.

When you add everything together, I'd say a $200,000 term policy, with your spouse as beneficiary, should do the job for most people. Of course, if you live in an expensive urban area, if you have kids in private schools, or if there are other unusual expenses, the amount of insurance would go up.

At age thirty, do you know what a $200,000 term policy would cost? Peanuts! Probably 80 cents per thousand, or $160 per year. That's nothing, absolutely nothing, when you consider the protection and peace of mind you get. But I should say right here that I do not favor ordinary or permanent life insurance. I consider it such a monstrous sting as a supposed "investment" that I'll devote the next chapter to my views on it.

Individual Retirement Accounts. Better known as IRAs, these are important vehicles that any wise investor, regardless of age, should select. I would urge you to go for the full $2,000 that's allowable each year. Under pending legislation, a nonemployee housewife would be allowed another $2,000, in contrast to the $250 originally allowed.

All that money, as I'm sure you know, can be excluded from your income in the year in which you make the investment. If the deposit is made before April 15 (or the due date of your tax return), the amount can be deducted from last year's income. In addition, the interest and other gains the IRA accrues are tax-free until your retirement, when, presumably, you will be in a lower income tax bracket. I consider the IRA to be such a major building block for an investment program, whether you're young or old, single or married, that we'll go into it in detail in a later chapter.

No-load mutual funds. After putting aside your "rainy-day money" and getting some life insurance and an IRA, you should take a look at a good no-load mutual fund. You can begin buying shares in one for as little as $100 monthly. As I've mentioned before, it enables you to take advantage of one of the major secrets of effective investment: diversification.

For investors who are younger than, say, thirty, I would suggest a growth fund rather than an income fund. These young people are at a stage in their life cycles when they can afford to take a little risk. Also, the compound growth possible with a growth fund can work in their favor over a long period of time. Older investors, especially those approaching retirement, may want to concentrate on funds that produce a consistent amount of interest. If carefully chosen, these bond or money-market shares don't place the underlying value of the capital investment at risk.

The choice of a mutual fund is directly related to the stage at which you find yourself in your life cycle. So let's now consider three stages in the typical life cycle. You will find yourself in one of these categories, but wherever you are, you'll have to tailor what I say to your own personal situation. That's part of the responsibility and the excitement of being an independent investor.

LIFE CYCLE STAGE I: THE YOUNG TURK

Let's consider first the investor who is thirty-five years old or younger. Suppose you're the farsighted sort who is already aware that it's best to prepare sooner rather than later for your children's education fifteen years from now. Or you're pointing toward a vacation home you want to enjoy. Or you're looking ahead toward retirement.

Specifically, assume you want to quit work at age sixty, by which time you and your wife will have no dependents. Exclusive of any pension and Social Security payments, you would like a $2,500 monthly return on your investments—or $30,000 yearly— to cover all major expenses and allow for a few luxuries. (The future erosion of the dollar through inflation may mean that this $2,500 monthly figure will be low for your needs. In any case, its important to figure inflation into future retirement income.)

This would amount to, say, 10 percent of $300,000, a conservative figure you can definitely achieve with proper planning. If you invest only $10,000 right now at 12 percent per annum, it will grow to more than $31,000 in ten years; to more than $96,000 in twenty years; and to only a few dollars less than $300,000 in thirty years.

A 12 percent yearly return isn't that much, by the way. Even at present money market interest rates, you can almost achieve that. And if you find one of the many good growth investments that are available, you can exceed that figure significantly. Healthy companies grow at healthy rates, and this growth is usually reflected in the increase in value of their stocks. IBM, for example, has a track record of about 20 percent growth per annum. Some of the high-growth companies have soared at even higher rates. For example, my own company has never grown at less than 50 percent per annum to date.

If you invest your $10,000 at age thirty, you can retire at sixty with about $300,000 of interest-bearing capital. But you should start saving even earlier than age thirty, if you can. For men and women between twenty-five and thirty-five, who are well into a first or second job, laying aside even a few dollars a month can be difficult. I know; I've been there myself.

But this is the very period in your life when the compounding effect is most powerful. So forget about buying that Porsche or taking that trip to Europe. Take an expensive vacation every other year, rather than yearly. Discipline yourself, and get started immediately! If you do, you'll be immeasurably pleased with your foresight, and with my good advice, five or ten years down the road.

A strong no-load, growth-oriented mutual is a good place to put most of your investment money in this first stage of your life cycle. If you can invest only $50 a month in such a fund, or $600 yearly, and you begin in your middle or even late twenties, the compounding effect will allow you to accumulate $10,000 rather easily by the time you are thirty-five. It's a good idea, by the way, to reinvest all dividends and capital gains that your fund earns for you. That way your investment will increase even more rapidly.

With a few years of investing experience behind you, you're becoming more aware of what's going on in your own company and other companies. You have been reading more financial publications, such as *Business Week*, *Fortune,* and *The Wall Street Journal.* Also, your practical experience in investing and your broad reading have given you a sense of the market's psychology and the movement of the market cycles. In a word, you are now becoming a mature independent investor.

As you become more knowledgeable when you near the end of this first stage in your life cycle, at about age thirty-five, you can start picking individual securities. But remember the basic principles and "secrets" we've discussed up to this point: Don't go after the first hot tip you hear. Sit down and do a little private study of several stock possibilities before you settle on any one.

My advice is never to put more than 10 percent of your total investment portfolio into any one security. If you have saved $8,000, perhaps $800 should be in one security. The other 90 percent might go into a diversified mutual fund or funds.

I've seen too many people plunge 50 percent of their total $8,000 into one security, and then the investment proves a washout. Their $4,000 investment drops to $2,000, and they lose 25 percent of their capital. In bear markets some inexperienced investors get so discouraged that they liquidate their entire portfolio, at the worst of times to sell out.

Of course, it's possible to become an investing monomaniac at the other extreme. While the chronic risk takers may sink all or much of their assets into one speculative stock, the most conservative among us sometimes plunge all they have into a bank savings account or a certificate of deposit. If you're older and approaching retirement, there may be some argument for this approach, but not when you're young and can take advantage of compounded growth.

Those who put all their money into fixed-income investments always miss out on the rapid first move of the next bull market. It often happens that this first leg, as we call it, or the first one-third of a brand-new upsurge moves with amazing speed. I remember one August only a few years ago when the market shot straight up, twenty to thirty points daily. Stocks were doubling and tripling in value in very short periods of time. In this kind of heady atmosphere things proceed so swiftly that even professional investors have a difficult time identifying exactly what's happening. Yet in those relatively brief periods, when stocks double and triple in value, an astute investor can make a killing and increase his personal holdings dramatically. If you're prepared, be poised to become just such an investor as the next stage in your life cycle begins.

LIFE CYCLE STAGE II: THE MIDDLE-AGED MOVER

Your second life-cycle period lies between the ages of thirty-five and fifty-five. During this phase you are well established in your career, and you probably have more dollars available for investment.

You should continue to put money into an IRA each year. But it's essential at this stage that you invest amounts well above the

IRA limit if you hope to achieve your ultimate financial goals, such as a comfortable retirement, education of your children, or buying that country house you've always wanted.

With your children getting older and the full burden of college education looming just ahead or already upon you, you'll want to moderate somewhat your degree of risk. Keep a third of your investments in liquid form, a third in securities, and a third in real estate.

The one-third, one-third, one-third division of your capital is suggested only as a general rule of thumb. I find it a little conservative and prefer to have 10 percent of my assets in liquid form, 30 percent in real estate (including my home), and 60 percent in securities. But that's just me. You may want to play it slightly more or less speculatively, depending on your special situation.

By the way, did it occur to you that owning your own home is one of the best possible tax shelters and investments you can have? It's not liquid, of course: You can't cash in, unless you go through the hassle of getting a second mortgage. But in an inflationary cycle residential real estate has proven to be one of the better forms of investment.

By this time in your life, if you've started early enough, you should be a bit more adept at spotting investment cycles, not only in this country but also abroad. There are international economies that are growing at a substantially higher rate than those of the United States and Europe. These include Japan, Hong Kong (at least, before the 1997 transfer to China), Singapore, and even Korea. For diversification you might get into some good mutual funds that hold stocks in foreign companies. Or perhaps you sense opportunities in precious metals, gold or silver. The safest way to get into these investments is to buy into fund groups that emphasize them, though I'm personally most unenthusiastic about precious metals and stones in any form.

You might even increase your investments in venture capital projects. I have recommended that, in general, it's a good idea—especially in the first phase of your investing experience—to limit your speculative investments to about 5 percent of your total holdings. But as you move into this second life cycle, earn more money, and gain more expertise in what to do with your money, you may want to increase this percentage to 10 percent or even a little more. These flyers might be in the form of limited partnerships in real estate. Or you might want to invest some of your capital in new, closely held corporations run by managements that are known to you.

These speculative holdings will satisfy a primitive urge we all have for excitement. Undoubtedly, there will be a few "comets" in your portfolio that go up like crazy and then, all of a sudden, plummet back down. I've had investments that have gone up tenfold before they crashed. If you can jump ship in time, fantastic! Occasionally, you'll get lucky with a holding that may go up and *stay* up, a happy circumstance that will substantially increase the size of your assets. Our own company went up 90 times in value, and it's still going strong.

Whatever happens, these risky flyers are all thrilling to watch. As long as you limit the percentage of your capital invested in these volatile ventures, you'll minimize the damage to your nerves. Even if your speculations decline to zero, you will still have 90 percent of your portfolio intact to give you comfort.

The key phrase in all this is, *Keep yourself disciplined!* Come up with a personal investment plan specifying the predetermined amounts you expect to go into each type of vehicle. Then sock that money away regularly as planned, without missing a beat.

Let's say that you are forty years old and looking forward to that retirement goal of about $300,000 at age sixty. If you are earning $40,000 to $50,000 a year and have an active family life, it won't be easy to put aside all you should save. You'll need to save about $4,000 to $5,000 yearly, at least in the first few years. It will take this kind of savings program for you to accumulate enough capital quickly enough so that the compounding effect can enable your holdings to "take off" toward your ultimate goal of $300,000. You'll have to bite the bullet a little and strongly discipline yourself.

Again, you should first get into an IRA, even to the extent of borrowing money to put into it. You'll thus be reducing your taxable income which means you are going to save $1,000 to $2,000 if you are in the 40–50 percent income tax bracket. You'll write off the interest you pay on the loan you took out, and your IRA returns are, of course, tax-deferred.

On the other hand, at age forty you are not going to reach your target of about $300,000 with government bonds that may pay 8 to 9 percent. Nor are you going to make it on corporate bonds at 10 percent. You're much better off going into growth securities, at least with a substantial part of your investments, and then reinvesting the capital gains and dividends. These companies should have an internal rate of return on their capital of 15 percent or more, compounded every year. That's what you hope to get in the stock market when you buy the common stocks of these growth companies. If I were you, I would put a quarter of my investments each year into mutual funds investing in such growth companies.

For those of you who made the mistake of putting your hard-earned dollars into cash-value life insurance, where the rate of return is unconscionably below market rates, this is an appropriate time to withdraw *all* your insurance cash value. Never mind the howls of protest you will receive from your insurance broker. Remember, he's a salesman and thinking of future commissions.

For example, at age forty you have perhaps a $20,000 whole-life policy that has accumulated $4,000 in cash value. Where do you think that $4,000 came from? Pennies from heaven? No, indeed. It came from your own premium payments.

So I would have a medical exam and make sure I still qualify for insurance, and then quickly buy a $200,000 term policy. At $1 per $1,000, this would cost you about $200 yearly. Also, it would be annually renewable until age seventy or eighty. Finally, I would close out my old whole-life policy and put all the cash value into one or two growth funds.

In addition to an unhealthy fixation on insurance, some forty-year-olds also focus too much on tax shelters. It's a mistake to end up in some oil and gas venture, a flaky windmill scheme, an obscure cattle-feeding operation, or a pie-in-the-sky solar energy deal that requires pure luck ever to turn a profit. Yes, you may save some money on taxes, but you won't get rich this way. Your primary focus should be on investments that are going to make you 12 percent or more a year, regardless of the tax consequences.

LIFE CYCLE STAGE III: THE OLDER CROWD

When you reach your fifties, whether you're a doctor, a lawyer, a business executive, a middle-level manager, or whatever your position, you're reaching the peak of your earning power. If you haven't put retirement funds aside regularly, this is the time when you *must* undertake a crash program to increase your assets. It may be a rude shock when you turn 55 to realize you haven't done a thing to prepare for retirement. But all is not lost.

One possibility is to cut way back on the discretionary items in your personal budget, such as entertainment and vacations, and put aside a large percentage out of each paycheck. The money you save should be invested mostly in secure investments; for the most part, that means those that are income-producing. Unfortunately, because you are at the top of your earning power, you'll be taxed heavily on ordinary savings accounts and money market funds. So you should look seriously at tax-exempt securities as the best parking place for your money.

Another approach to investing during this third stage of your life cycle, if you haven't been putting money away right along, is to push your retirement well back beyond sixty, perhaps all the way to seventy, the legal limit. That way you'll add years to your earning power, and you'll have more time to accumulate a nest egg, above and beyond your expected pension and Social Security payments.

If you have failed to establish an independent investing program up to this point, you can't possibly make up completely for lost time. That's a hard thing to accept, but you'll just have to accept it. Then resolve to proceed conservatively, with as much capital as you can get together.

Above all, don't panic and start taking unreasonable chances with the money you do have in the hope of catching up. I've seen so many people end up in disaster by desperately taking additional risks, only to stumble into the worst possible situation right on the eve of retirement.

This third and last stage of the life cycle is the time to consolidate your previous gains. You should begin to put more of your funds into the most secure investments, and plan your transition to a world of reduced work. It is not the time to turn into a hotshot high-roller.

There is at least one group that I haven't mentioned here, those lucky men and women who operate their own little businesses.

They can create a nice income for themselves during their most productive years, and they have many tax advantages and a great deal more personal flexibility than those who are locked into a regular salary. But sometimes these people tend to forget to set up IRAs for their own retirement programs. They also overlook, until it's almost too late, the all-important fact that unless they can unload the business for a bundle when they reach retirement age, they'll be strapped in their effort to generate continuing income.

I've always believed in the old saw about investing a considerable amount of money in your own enterprise, especially in the early stages, when it's just getting off the ground. Yes, it does involve putting most or all of your eggs in one basket, but unlike other investments, you make *very* sure that you watch that basket carefully when you run your own business.

Having presented this overview of approaches to investing at different stages of life, I want to spend a little more time, as I promised, discussing one aspect of your financial plan, your insurance program. I feel so strongly about the importance of avoiding permanent life insurance that I devoted the next chapter to it.

7

A Plague on Permanent
Life Insurance!

THE LIFE INSURANCE INDUSTRY has, for many years, grossly abused us Americans. I've already paid my disrespects to it in brief. Now, let me flesh out the scandalous indictment.

With an incredible incentive system for the salesmen, it seems that the worse a life insurance policy is for a client, the better it is for the insurance company and the agent. That is, the higher the amount of money that goes into the company, the lower the coverage for the customer. Also, the higher the cost for the customer per $1,000 of coverage, the higher the commission and compensation to the company.

Even worse, some of the companies flirt with fraud in the way they sell insurance on fear, rather than on the basis of what it really is—the *possibility* of premature death.

As I discussed in the last chapter, if you have no dependents or family responsibilities, there is almost no need for life insurance except for the minimal costs of disposal and burial. On the other hand, as you go through your life cycle, with marriage, children, and others becoming dependent on you, there is certainly need for life insurance. But the most advantageous way to cover yourself is by what we call *annual renewable term life insurance*. Unfortunately, this is not the product that insurance agents try hardest to sell.

Agents do handle term, but it will be the last thing that they pull out of their bag of tricks. Why? Because it carries the lowest commissions for them.

Back in 1959 I worked for several months for a life insurance company. Their training program was my first in-depth exposure to life insurance. I was an extremely poor salesman; in fact, I never sold a policy—I didn't have the heart. Finally, by mutual agreement, I left the company. But in the sixty days of training I learned a lot about the inner workings of life insurance companies. These are basically marketing organizations that get young people to sell high-cost policies to their friends and relatives first.

One thing the insurance sales instructors failed to tell me is that when a person buys a $10,000 policy of "ordinary" or "permanent" or "whole" life, it's really a decreasing term life policy, coupled with an increasing, low-interest savings account. This means that each year your life insurance protection goes down as your "cash value" (savings account) increases. Moreover, in those days the cash value portion accumulated through interest at the magnificent rate of about 2.5 percent. Finally, the agents consistently neglected to tell the prospective client that there is no buildup of cash value in the first two years, because during that period all the premiums are paid out in commissions to the salesmen.

That's not all. The company, in their training program, tried to convince the salesmen that we were selling $10,000 worth of life insurance that was truly "permanent." But that's a misnomer. You see, when the customer reaches the age of seventy or seventy-five and his policy's cash value equals the face value of the policy, with no more premiums due, there is *no* insurance involved. Any insurance coverage is finished. All that's left is just the cash value—the enforced, low-interest savings account—that the customer has accumulated through his premiums. In other words, if the client dies, it's his own money that his heirs will be getting back. They'll receive nothing at all from the company. What's more, if the holder of the policy has taken out a loan on his cash value and he dies while the loan is outstanding, the amount paid to the beneficiary will be reduced by the amount of the loan.

Not surprisingly, I've always felt a deep-seated aversion to the industry since my training days, and it isn't just because I was a poor salesman. The problem, from my viewpoint, is that they have been selling *fear* to the public, and they have not presented the so-called permanent insurance for what it really is.

What 99 percent of all cash-value policies really are, as I've said, is a decreasing term policy with a cash buildup. The buildup of cash, or what they call your cash value, occurs because you're paying excessive premiums that you wouldn't have to pay under a more equitable system.

Let me illustrate what I mean. Here you are at age thirty, and you buy a $10,000 policy. The first two years there's no cash buildup, mainly because the salesman is taking his commissions. After that the cash buildup increases so that perhaps by age sixty-five it's worth $7,500.

If you die at sixty-five, your beneficiary gets $7,500 of *your* cash value. The remainder of the $10,000, or $2,500, comes from the company. You had only $2,500 of coverage when you passed on. Yet the insurer has the gall to call this "permanent" life insurance! Every year, your coverage is going down as your cash value goes up, until eventually there's nothing in the policy except your own money. A lucrative deal for the insurance company, perhaps, but not a great deal for you.

And remember this: As you're building up your cash value by putting in high-priced premiums at low interest, the insurance company isn't making the same mistake. They, of course, go out into the open market and make a bundle on your money at rates that are far higher than what they are paying out. For example, they might pay you 3 percent while they get 9 or 10 percent on the same money.

Just a few years ago, under consumer pressure and know-how, the industry began to modernize a bit. But millions and millions of dollars had already been squandered on this "permanent" junk. The insurance company got all the money, and middle Americans got ripped off. Some of these decent and trusting souls were left without enough money for retirement because they had used their extra cash to pay insurance premiums.

So when it comes to buying life insurance, the best thing is to shop around for term policies. You should ask for "guaranteed annual renewable" term insurance, which will allow you to remain insured indefinitely, regardless of changes in your medical condition. Such policies are inexpensive, and the more you buy, the lower the rate (per $1,000 of coverage). But be prepared for resistance if you go to a regular agency. Your salesman will argue vigorously, "Oh, my goodness! You shouldn't buy term because every year your premiums will go up. You should get this permanent life policy if you want to keep the same amount of protection later at the same premium."

Your reply: "Nonsense! First of all, as I grow older, my need for insurance usually declines. Secondly, the whole life or permanent life is just a form of decreasing term. The amount of insurance is steadily dropping as my cash value increases.

"Also, if I die with a loan on my policy [though not everyone takes out such a loan], the loan will be subtracted from what my beneficiary gets. I am forced to borrow on my *own money*, and the amount my beneficiary gets declines!

"In any case, my term policy is guaranteed renewable each year until I decide I don't need insurance coverage. So you see why I say 'nonsense'!"

The best thing an agent could do for you as a client would be to sell you a lot more coverage in the form of term insurance when you have the most responsibilities protecting your spouse and children. The price would be relatively low, and the returns to your beneficiary would amount to much more. Unfortunately, this just doesn't happen.

But you can beat the insurance game by going to savings banks that offer good term insurance. Or you can check out the ads in *The Wall Street Journal* or other sources for low-cost term. Sometimes, your credit card or other memberships will offer you low-cost term at group rates. To find the best deal, just compare the dollar rate per $1,000 of coverage. Of course, you want to be sure that any policy you take out is from a company that's rated A-plus, A, or B-plus. To this end, you can insist that the agent give you the rating of his company. If it checks out, then you're okay.

You'll come out ahead if you apply for a new policy every so often. I do this myself on a regular basis because over the past twenty years the standard mortality tables have improved substantially, allowing you substantial savings on insurance, even though you're older. So it behooves you to make another application at no cost, with a free medical exam thrown in. If you don't get a better rate or if you prove uninsurable for some reason, just hold on to your old policy.

I first started buying term life in my middle twenties, when I had my first child. Now, in my middle forties, I'm paying about the same rate per $1,000 of insurance that I paid back then. This is at least one nice thing I can say about an industry that all too often grows fat by "insuring" you with your own money.

Let me leave you with this final, important thought: Life insurance is simply not a vehicle for investing. Neither are annuities. The returns don't measure up to what you can get with a wise strategy in the stock market.

Now let's drop the negatives and return to the positive side of being an independent investor. You want to make some money in the market, and that means you have to do some research. The first place to start—and in some ways the most intimidating—is the corporate literature that is supposed to tell what a company and its stock are all about.

8

A Crash Course in Gobbledygook

EVERY CALLING boasts a special vocabulary of its own: law, medicine, the different branches of science, and even holy orders. The financial community is no exception. In fact, it's worse. It's private language is an unholy hash of economics, accounting, and "legalese." Reading a prospectus makes the ordinary tenant's lease seem like a third-grade reader.

If you're dealing with a company already traded on the exchange, the prospectus is somewhat thinner and easier to wade through. On the other hand, if it's a brand-new company, I defy the average investor to make much sense out of the complicated verbiage in the corporate literature.

But don't despair. Here's a short "course" I have prepared to make you an expert in speed-reading such formidable material.

The first bit of advice will save you a lot of time: Take any prospectus a broker sends you on new issues—that is, companies that are about to go public—and throw it in the wastebasket. Unless, you are a large customer of the broker, you're better off not wasting your time trying to read such material.

Oh, yes, it may seem fun and exciting at first, to get what seems to be an "inside track" on some new company that the general public doesn't know about; but the small investor usually ends up being notified of as many bad issues as good ones, and the really great ones are going to be snapped up by the broker's preferred customers, the large institutional investors. They'll always crowd out the little fellow on this kind of investment. In this case, bigger is definitely better.

Let me make myself crystal clear here: The likelihood of you, the average investor, even getting a good hunk of a great company is practically zilch. There's a much better chance you will wind up with a good hunk of a real disaster. On the other hand, if you know someone in a company that is about to go public and you get on a new-issues list that way, you may want to wait a few minutes before you toss the prospectus away. It may still be a dog, but then again, it may be the best deal you've ever been offered in your life. So do some selective reading.

First, determine exactly what business is involved. This is especially important if you don't know too much about a company because it has been operating as a closed corporation and is about to go public. You'll usually find that statement on the first or second page of the prospectus. If it's a hamburger business, the literature will say so. If the company is in the publishing business or produces computer software, that information will be there as well.

So, right off the bat you can find out exactly what kind of an industry you're dealing with. That will help you decide whether you want to go any farther. For example, your reading in general financial publications may have convinced you that a certain type of computer is past its prime in the marketplace. Then you'll want to avoid companies that deal in this item. As for me, at the moment I don't think I would continue reading a small computer company's prospectus.

The next point you want to look for will be on page 3 or 4. There you'll find a five-year history of key financial data. I would then study the company's revenues in relation to its earnings growth rate to determine that aspect of its performance.

A good question at this stage of your reading is, Has the business been profitable? So take a long, hard look at its earnings per share as a closed corporation over a period of several years, and then compare those earnings with the expected public offering price.

Personally, none of this information will usually be decisive for me, but at least it gives me a general feel for the company. If all the figures add up to something truly exciting, I may even buy it. But this type of investment would fit into the category of speculation. In other words, it would have to be part of that 5 to 10 percent of my portfolio that I want to have some fun with, but which I don't mind losing completely, if it so happens.

Let me conclude this consideration of new issues with some personal observations. I first started "playing" with new issues in 1960–61, and it seemed the easiest way to make money. In that period stocks would come out at $10 and go to $15 or $20 almost overnight. It was almost too easy, like betting on a fixed race.

But it was also quite evident to anyone who knew the brokerage business that brokers used these issues for several reasons: (1) They allocated small amounts to their best customers; (2) they allocated some to brand-new customers to get their business for the future; and (3) they used them to make up for bad issues they had offered in the past.

These new-issue phases only come every two to three years. One of the last, as of this writing, was April to June of 1983. In that period almost every public issue went above the offering price during the first day of public sales.

Unfortunately, one price you pay for the few good shares you get is that you are put under an obligation to buy other issues from that same salesman. Often, that means you're encouraged to buy his lemons as well as his sweetest sales. It's not an obligation that's in writing, but it's presented as a strong emotional and moral obligation.

The broker might say, "Come on now, if you want this new, sure-profit deal, you may also want to consider this tax shelter I'm offering. Our relationship is a real relationship!"

The idea is that you have to buy the bad or marginal issues in order to get the good ones. This happened to me a number of times when I first started out, and it took me a while to understand what was happening. Sometimes, I would do well for a while in a new issue, but then the bottom would drop out and I'd lose almost everything I had gained.

When the market decline of 1962 hit, I got clobbered on a number of new issues. At that time I got caught up in the obligation thing, where I bought a new issue and felt obligated to buy sizable amounts of the same broker's losers. On the really hot issues, it was quite limited as to what I could buy; I might be allowed to purchase only 25 shares or so. I remember when Comsat went public. It came out at 20, and I got just a few hundred shares. This was a good investment, but the bad issues I bought along with it wiped out the Comstat profits.

Here's the way the new-issue procedure works: Typically, you might buy the new issue at $20 a share. Then it will usually start trading at a price above the first price. But suppose you want to get out of the stock for some reason? Many brokers get upset if you try to sell the issue back through their firm because they lose their fees if this happens. And you're *really* a bad guy if you sell the same issue back to them at the same price or at a loss. They may even try to imply you're behaving unethically. In such a case, the typical advice from the broker will be an urgent whisper: "Don't sell through me! Sell it back through another broker!" That way, he gets to keep his commission.

In my opinion, you should be able to sell any new issue back if you want. But expect the broker to resist with every weapon of persuasion at his command because of the large commissions on new issues—perhaps four to six times the normal fees on an ordinary stock transaction. Never forget that there is a built-in incentive for the brokers to sell them. Sometimes, by the way, the commissions are built into the price of the new-issue shares, and the broker may try to convince you there is no commission. But don't you believe it!

In conclusion, I'd say that reading a prospectus on new issues *may* have some merit in some circumstances. Usually, however, it's just a waste of time. In a similar vein, reading an annual report may be a waste of time unless you go about it the right way.

My advice is this: If you want to spend your reading time gainfully, study the annual reports of those companies in which you already have an interest. They can provide a feel for the business because they contain important highlighted information, photographs of company activity, and even some explanations that may offer clear insights into what is happening to the enterprise.

The first thing I look for in an annual report is the financial results and trends. I always ask myself, "Is there a clearly healthy trend over at least a five-year period, given the movements of the outside economy and the stock market cycles during the same span of time?"

Then, I assess the product lines, which are usually described in some detail. Does my personal experience and reading suggest that these lines will be strong and profitable over the next few years? For example, if I notice that a company specializing in exercise facilities focuses on old-fashioned rubber shimmying equipment rather than modern aerobics or "pumping iron," I'd probably steer clear of that company.

But I don't just let my reading of annual reports go at that. I would urge you to subscribe to a financial service that provides summaries of many companies' annual reports. These include publications by such companies as the Value Line Investment Survey and Standard & Poor's and will cost about $360 a year. If you don't want to pay that much, you can find this same information in the financial sections of most public libraries.

"But why," you may protest, "should I go to all this effort when I can rely on the expertise of a securities analyst in a brokerage firm?"

Having been an analyst myself, I certainly don't want to rain on their parade; but they are not omniscient, not by a long shot. Also, when you rely on just one of them, you're violating one of the basic rules we discussed a few pages back. Remember: It's important always to seek the counsel of at least two investment advisers, and this includes advice that comes in writing.

There are other problems with these analysts. Often they rely on the company itself for their basic information. Obviously, no executive will divulge to them adverse facts if he can possibly avoid it. In addition, to retain good rapport with the company, analysts sometimes are more gentle than they should be in their appraisals.

I'll go even farther and suggest that in some instances there may be totally indefensible, crass motives that reside in your seemingly gracious and objective analyst. Let's say that an analyst for a brokerage house sees a company's prospects through rose-tinted glasses and makes an overly optimistic estimate of its potential earnings. It's more than coincidence, isn't it, that such estimates make it far easier for the salesmen in the analyst's brokerage firm to peddle that particular stock?

I'm only suggesting that you, as an *independent* investor, take analysts' estimates *cum grano salis*. Don't accept them as infallible gurus, even though they are touted as "specialists" in certain types of issues. There is altogether too much "guruism" in the financial world, too many overrated experts, too many self-anointed prophets.

Listen to advice from any and every source, to be sure, but make up your own mind independently. Don't play follow-the-leader. If you have any doubts about this approach, talk to some of Joe Granville's clients.

9

The Best Little Stock Market
School in the World

You won't find it in a catalog of business schools. Nor will you find it in the training courses of any brokerage house. No, the very best place for you to begin a practical education that will make you piles of money in the market is right where you're sitting now—and that's probably in your own home.

You don't need an MBA, not even a bachelor's in economics or business, to become a reasonably successful independent investor. But you *do* need the modest weekly application of your own time, perhaps an hour or two a day, at least at first. And you will need to exercise a great deal of common sense.

I recommend the following eight steps for anyone who wants to graduate from rank amateur to market-savvy investor:

Step 1: Read the financial pages of your local newspaper every day.

As you begin to follow the activities of various companies and study their daily quotations, it's amazing how quickly these abstract, once-dull figures come alive. You find yourself getting absorbed in the ups and downs of the market. Moreover, rather than wait for the roundup in the next morning's newspaper, you will find yourself listening to radio reports shortly after the market's close each day.

Step 2: Put your money on the line.

Thus far you have been engaged in a dry run, maybe making an occasional mental investment and following a certain stock in its rise or fall. This isn't enough. As quickly as you can, take a nominal sum, such as $1,000, and actually invest it. This enables you to progress from the play money of "Monopoly" to the real thing.

I would advise buying two $500 blocks of two different stocks that have caught your eye, or maybe $1,000 worth of no-load mutual funds. Don't enter the market with the defeatist attitude that you're going to lose. Play the investing game with great optimism. Starting modestly, you need not worry about losing a large percentage on your first foray. Consider any small loss as a "tuition fee" in the good old S.O.H.K. (School Of Hard Knocks).

Step 3: Do even more financial reading of a national newspaper.

After your first modest investment, I suspect, you will want to follow the market in greater depth. For Monday-to-Friday reading I recommend *The Wall Street Journal*, the premier national newspaper for business news. You don't have to read it cover to cover; just concentrate on the highlights. The new *Investor's Daily* is also informative. The financial section of *USA Today* is quite good, as are the business pages of *The New York Times*, *The Los Angeles Times*, and *The Chicago Tribune*.

I read *The Wall Street Journal* faithfully for a good half hour every morning—from the back to the front!

After a two-minute scan of the major events appearing in the left-hand summary column on page one, I go immediately to the last pages, which show what the stock prices did the previous day. The back section also contains many of the trend charts we talk about in this book.

I don't pretend you must read everything. You just can't; so you must learn to skim what's relevant and skip what's not. Even though the market moves in long bull and bear cycles, you should definitely glance at the page one news summary of the events that may have had at least a temporary effect on the prices of your stocks. The more you match up the events, reports, and fears of the day with the stock prices, the more you'll develop a sense of how the all-important psychology of the market operates.

As for the feature and news articles in the *Journal*, look for the ones that cover your areas of interest, where you may invest in the future. Skip the others.

Step 4: Do still more reading of select magazines.

It's wise to subscribe to at least one investors' magazine. I consider *Forbes* and *Money* as probably the two best and most comprehensive magazines for the typical investor. I don't mean to slight periodicals like *Fortune, Business Week,* or *Barron's,* all of which are quite interesting and helpful. They carry broad-brush financial articles and narrow-focus pieces on specific companies that can be very revealing, if they happen to be within your special sphere of interest. But because there's so much good reading matter out there, you must force yourself to read only those publications and articles pertinent to you, while merely skimming or even ignoring the others. Too often, the freshman investor wallows in one article after another and winds up badly confused.

In the course of a year I read something out of practically all the magazines, even going so far as to dip into the *Harvard Business Review*. But this is not essential for a personal investing program. Just cram all the key items you can into a reading program that takes about five hours every week.

Step 5: Yes, more reading of key books on the market.

To avoid an emotional, frantic approach to the market, it would be prudent to dip into some of the fine old books that impart the flavor of speculation as it has been exercised down through the ages.

I immediately think of historical volumes like *Extraordinary Popular Delusions and the Madness of Crowds,* written in the 1850s. It describes precisely what the title says, the delusions of crowds throughout history. Also, the book analyzes the psychology of human movements, which, of course, is the basis of the psychology of the stock market.

Whenever we get too excited about one thing, be it the tulip mania in Holland two hundred years ago or the more recent boom in computer stocks, we must remember to take a long step backward and say, "Look, I'm getting dangerously emotional about this thing. I've got to cool it." If you achieve this detached, philosophical approach, you will avoid the most common pitfall of the sheeplike crowds who make ineffectual, fitful attempts to invest. They inevitably try unsuccessfully to buy at the low and sell at the high. They fail to understand that great oracle of the exchanges, "Know thyself and ignore the insanity of the market!"

For further reading I would recommend *Confessions of a Stock Market Operator,* written under a pen name by Jesse Livermore, the so-called boy wonder of the 1920s. On a more current note, as a no-load mutual fund enthusiast, I like William Donoghue's excellent *No-Load Mutual Fund Guide.*

There are many other volumes that would be helpful. For example, I'd recommend anything written by Charles Rolo, former *Money* magazine editor; also, Gerald Loeb's *Battle for Investment Survival* is worthwhile. Here are two others I like that are put out by one reliable investment publisher, Dow Jones–Irwin: *The Dow Jones-Irwin Guide to Using the Wall Street Journal,* by Michael B. Lehmann; and *Words of Wall Street: 2,000 Investment Terms Defined,* by Allan H. Pessin and Joseph A. Ross.

In addition, there are dozens of fine books available by mail, at any well-stocked bookstore, or at your local public library. I just have one broad reservation about your financial library. Perhaps I'm too practical, but I would stay away from the heavy, academic tomes. They'll tend to confuse you, and most likely the authors don't know a thing about how to turn a buck in the frenetic reality of the market. In fact, some of these professors have probably never bought or sold a share of stock in their lives.

In contrast, you could easily be in my position with just a few years of hands-on investing experience. I've bought thousands of securities and sold as many, and I've used more than one hundred stockbrokers. So, as an honors graduate of the good old School Of Hard Knocks, I feel qualified to pass this rather harsh judgment on most of the academics who survey the market from atop their ivory towers.

Step 6: Now you may be ready to try a formal course somewhere.

I'd never recommend that you head for a classroom until you've done plenty of reading and investing on your own. Otherwise, you'll lose your independence and individuality, and you'll tend to do whatever the teacher says, rather than what is best for you personally.

But after you have a little background, so that you can approach critically what's presented in a formal course, you may want to enroll somewhere. Many of the country's fine junior colleges offer introductory evening classes in personal financial planning and other aspects of money management. These can give you some good ideas about how to keep records of your investments.

That's an important feature of being a good money manager: You should have a notebook or ledger in which you enter all your purchases and sales, with dates, amounts of capital, commissions, gains, and losses. That way you can see how you're really doing on any given investment at any point in time.

There are also some good correspondence courses, but most of them require a lot of time. Actually, you can obtain much the same information by reading some of the books I've mentioned. But whatever approach you choose, don't forget to stay practical. Don't just sit in your easy chair and read. Get out into the market and invest!

If you buy a Ford, you'll always read the Ford ads and articles on Fords afterward. Buy a Sony, and it's the same thing. Buy stock in a company, and you'll start reading anything related to that company. Make a small commitment with your money, and you'll find that your mind will follow your pocketbook.

Just one added suggestion on this subject of outside education: You may want to join an investment club or association instead of going to a junior or community college. In my opinion, these clubs can be even more helpful than many courses because you have much more of an opportunity to bounce ideas off practical investors like yourself.

Step 7: Consider subscribing to an investment advisory service.

I say "consider" because I regard this step as optional, in part because services put out by companies like Value Line and Standard & Poor's can be rather expensive. But an advisory service could provide a good transition from your position as a rank beginner to your eventual status as a truly independent investor.

Frankly, I think most people should be able to skip this step. But if your ambition is to become a quasi-professional investor, there are quite a few good professional services available. The trick is to shop around and find the publications that fit you and your particular investment style and objectives.

You might look in *Barron's* or *Forbes* for some possibilities. Or, better yet, if you can find a friend who has had a good experience with such a firm, take out a trial subscription and see how you like it.

You're looking, most of all, for integrity and objectivity. Then you want to know something about the history of your potential advisory service so that you can examine its track record and determine how effective it is. The services are all different, so this is going to take a bit of research on your part. But the right one is there, at a cost-effective price, if you feel you need the help.

Step 8: Take all advice with a grain of salt.

Since I have just given good investment advisory services as much of a plug as I'll give anybody, this cautionary note may sound contradictory. But the old rule of *cum grano salis* should be applied nevertheless. In the final analysis, if you are going to be an independent investor, the decision has to be yours.

By all means listen to advice, as long as it's coming from someone independent of the transaction, someone who has no monetary interest in what you buy. Perhaps I shouldn't go so far as to say, "Never listen to a stockbroker." But in the large majority of cases, the best, most impartial advice you can find most definitely will not come from him.

It boggles the mind to imagine how many investors don't know what they are doing out there, and how many stockbrokers are taking advantage of them by "churning" their accounts—that is, the brokers are constantly persuading the gullibles to buy or sell.

I can't repeat often enough the obvious and sordid fact that most of us usually forget: A broker and his brokerage firm *only* make money when someone buys or sells. To accomplish this, they play upon our basest instincts: the desire to make a quick buck, and fear.

The easiest way to persuade a customer to buy is to give him some strong hope or even a promise that he will make money. Here, brokers rely on the quick-buck motive. The easiest way to persuade a client to sell is to warn direly that the market is going down, down, down. The emotion they're playing on now? You guessed it—fear.

In point of fact, most brokers-salesmen aren't really suited to be objective advisers. Their interest in selling you as much as possible makes it impossible for them to be true fiduciaries in handling your money. Also, they have little understanding of or experience in the psychology of the market. Many of them are very young, and if they don't make it fairly quickly on commissions, they're out. As a result, you find a fairly high turnover in the business.

In the *up* markets, the brokers get hired in droves; in the *down* markets, they leave en masse. A number of my friends in my 1961 graduating class at Stanford Business School went into the brokerage business. If even 5 percent of them are still in it today, I would be flabbergasted.

What happens—and you can check this against your own painful experiences—is that the average broker is a highly persuasive, confident sort of fellow, all of which adds up to being a good salesman. But brokers are also as subject as most of their clients to the emotions of the market. When the market is on the *up* side, commission-brokers themselves get caught up in the frenzy. They're aggressive and exuberant, and all this misguided and uninformed confidence spills over to the customer.

In the *down* markets, the opposite is true. They become quite depressed because, like any other human being, they don't like to recommend bad stocks. Also, their highly touted buys have collapsed in price. It's deflating to be proven wrong after you've made so many promises and persuaded your customers to put so much of their money on the line.

The eight steps presented in this chapter are not a one-shot route to a "degree" that certifies you as a know-it-all. You're not supposed to do some reading, get some advice, and then quit. No, the kind of "course" I'm talking about in this chapter is an ongoing affair. Your education in investments should be a continuing, evolving process.

By having a modest amount invested, you will naturally search for more information about the stock, fund, or other security you've chosen. You'll have a built-in motivator, nothing less than your own money that has been placed on the line. Your education will then proceed by leaps and bounds. Eventually, the only danger you'll have to guard against is the old failing that plagues all of us at one time or another, the sin of pride.

Shortly after taking my master's degree in 1961, which included a 120-page paper on the aluminum industry, I fancied myself as knowing a lot about that particular industry. Since I had also been dabbling in stocks since age thirteen, I was sure I knew an incredible amount about the stock market in general. I didn't. The market knew a lot more than I did, and it proceeded to make a fool of me. I had overlooked a number of basics, such as the general euphoric psychology that was building among many investors. I assumed that my investments were immune to the historic responses in the wake of waves of investor emotion.

But I turned out to be dead wrong. I was rather adept at doing fundamental analyses of individual companies, including cogent evaluations of such factors as balance sheets and product lines. But I didn't understand that everything, including excellent companies, goes down in a bad bear market. Therefore, I invested in several good companies, but I lost a bundle because I invested at the wrong phase of the overall market cycle.

But even with similar disappointments, your education can be a fun process. It's just a matter of learning not to become too cocky or too sure that you know all there is to know about any aspect of investing. Always retain a wary feeling that there *may* be something you don't know, something that's about to catch up to you and teach you a tough but important lesson.

Sure, that euphoric feeling of invincible self-assuredness is delightful, but so unprofitable. Accept the fact that many things you have not anticipated will happen, and that there must always be uncertainty. Such an attitude will make you a much stronger investor as you avoid becoming overconfident and overcommitted to any one stock. Investing in the stock market is much like any other discipline of life, such as physics or astronomy or anthropology. The more you know about it, the less it seems you really know.

And so ends my commencement address to you, as you receive your diploma from the S.O.H.K. Sure, you've perhaps lost a few thousand along the line, but compare this tuition fee with what a year at Harvard or Stanford would cost—$12,000 or so at this writing. And even if you paid that much money for such a high-falutin education, you wouldn't get as much useful knowledge anywhere as you have from the old School of Hard Knocks.

10

Some Inside Schwab Scoop on Selecting Individual Stocks and Bonds

ALL RIGHT, it was a dream—I admit it—but a lovely dream, and I almost pulled it off.

Back in 1961, when I was fresh out of business school and a budding securities analyst, I loved to play with slide rules. (Calculators weren't generally available in those days.) The magical number for me was 26—a whopping 26 percent growth rate per annum. I lived, breathed, ate, and drank that number.

I knew that if I could achieve that rate of increase on my personal assets, my money would grow tenfold every ten years. So, if in my twenties I got together only $1,000, in thirty years, by the time I was in my mid-fifties, I would be a millionaire!*

There were companies in those days growing at that rate, and there are still plenty today that grow that fast. It was and is just a matter of finding them. For a number of years I kept right on

---

*Figure it out yourself: set the "constant" button on your calculator for 1.26, enter 1,000, and press the multiplication button thirty times. The result: $1,025,927 and change!

target, even with occasional setbacks like my losses in 1962. But I was galloping, it seemed, toward my shining goal.

Then came the debacle. I was buffeted by some heavy bear markets, where I lost almost everything, and I had to start all over again. It was quite upsetting at the time, but I've since learned there was nothing unusual about my experience. In fact, I learned some important lessons.

First, for those who are young and have years to retrieve their losses if things go wrong, some risk is justified. Inevitably, there are going to be losses, but the possible reward from striving for higher rates of return balances the risk that inevitably goes along with such aggressiveness.

The second lesson, though, is different. It can be summed up in the word *caution*. Anyone who is putting together a portfolio should be thinking over the long term as well as the short. It makes no sense to earn a lot of money one year if you're going to lose it all the next.

So it's necessary to take some chances early in the game, but wise to put aside some of your winnings in investments that will weather the changing winds of the highly emotional market. One way to do this is to diversify your holdings among a variety of investment vehicles that will respond in different ways to different types of markets.

So if you're interested in individual securities, as most investors are at one time or another, what type should you choose? There's such a bewilderingly fat menu to pick from:

You have common stocks and preferred stocks . . . convertible preferred stocks . . . regular bonds and convertible bonds . . . warrants . . . options, including puts and calls . . . straddles . . . spreads . . . butterflies . . . futures . . . federal, state, and municipal bonds.

Before detailing the pluses and minuses of some of these forms of investment, let me offer a brief checklist:

- *Common stock*—the best vehicle to ride for growth, and 26 percent yearly *is* obtainable, if you know what you're doing.
- *Preferred stock*—not for the average investor. For corpora-

tions, there's a sweet tax incentive because the dividends of these preferred are 85 percent tax-free, but only for the corporations, not for individuals.

- *Corporate bonds*—no better than the company behind them. This form of investment may sound reassuring for the timid, but the company offering them might run into problems. If you stick to bonds rated B-plus to A, you should be safe enough, but the value of the bonds may fluctuate and you may find yourself locked into low returns if general interest rates go up.
- *U.S. government bills, notes, and bonds*—as safe as there is, but you'll never get rich. In fact, you won't even break even if inflation gets out of hand again.
- *State issues and municipals*—next to Uncle Sam in safety, except that some of the cities backing them may be in trouble. You have to check out the financial health of the municipalities. Also, there isn't much liquidity—except at excruciating discounts—in these holdings if you need to sell.
- *Puts, calls, and options*—they have their uses, both for speculation and as hedges for the prudent investor. But unless you *really* know what you're doing, don't play in this game!
- *Spreads, butterflies, etc.*—for the big boys and the crazies, not for you.

Now, for a bit more detail about some of these possibilities. Let's begin with common stocks.

THE CRAZY WORLD OF COMMON STOCKS

A complex world of fantasy has grown up around the stock market, especially with regard to trading in equities, or common stocks. One of the reasons for the mystique around these securities can be traced to their basic nature: They give the buyer part ownership in a business, with all the risks and potential rewards that this status entails. The fortunes that are made and lost on the various exchanges often involve those who trade common stocks more than other securities.

If you buy and sell for just a few months, you'll pick up many of the catch phrases, street "wisdom," and old-wives' tales of Wall Street, and most of the scuttlebutt is absolute nonsense.

For example, there's a silly shibboleth in the market world that goes, "You never go broke taking a profit!" Sounds logical, doesn't it? But for the individual investor who is trying to maximize his portfolio, there is an unsettling corollary: "You'll never get rich either!"

Suppose your broker calls you up and excitedly reports, "Good news. You're up three points. Maybe we ought to get out of this thing." A terse, two-letter response is appropriate in most cases: "No!"

There's another hoary slogan that I would like to debunk right now: "Only buy stocks that are ten times earnings." Ridiculous! As I've said before, pay little attention to the P/E ratio if you find a stock that appeals to you as having a promising future.

The point I'm trying to get across is that most catch phrases posing as unbreakable rules defeat the essence of a proper market strategy, flexibility. I can't emphasize that word too much. To illustrate, let me give you another painful example from my own experience.

In the spring of 1961 I wanted to buy some stock in American Photocopy, the original company that handled photocopy machines. My analyses and my gut feeling told me it was a comer. It was then selling for a little over $18 a share, and I put in a limit order to buy at 18. Remember, a *limit order* is one that can be executed only at the exact price and amount that the buyer specifies.

I had heard a lot about the importance of discipline, of sticking to a decision about a stock once you had made it. That was my slogan for the moment, accepted without regard for the countervailing principle of the importance of remaining flexible. I resolved to hang tough and not budge until that stock dipped to the level where I thought I should buy it.

Well, the stock came down to 18⅛, hovered there, and then recovered, but I didn't buy it. I lost out, of course. Furthermore, I had the painful experience of watching it go up in the next five months to 60, and finally it shot up above 60. By then I was too depressed to keep following its meteoric rise.

All my analyses about the company had proven correct, all my visions were justified, but I had lost out because of a lousy, narrow ⅛ of a point, or just 12.5 cents per share! A sorry shibboleth, a distorted notion about exercising discipline in placing orders, had shackled me, and I lost out on a huge profit, maybe even a small fortune.

I suppose you can call my action either stubbornness or stupidity. I call it stupidity, and I must say that many, many investors have proven themselves equally stupid by exercising what they think is self-discipline, but what in reality is rigidity. That's a cardinal sin in the investment world, whether it involves stocks, bonds, or options.

I learned something else from the American Photocopy disaster. The fury that I felt, the total brunt of my massive anger, was all directed at myself, and I had to live with it by myself. You may have a bitter memory of a loss, but the stock market has no memory of you. In fact, no one else in the world does, unless it happens to be those of your family or friends who shared in the loss as well.

I soon came to understand that I had to achieve the courage of a professional gambler who accepts the spin of the wheel with stoicism and regards the roll of the dice philosophically. Self-destructive rage or panic has no part in the common-stock game. You've got to pick yourself up and turn your attention to the next challenge. If you wallow in self-pity or continue to replay your past mistakes, you'll never develop the steel nerves you need to succeed as an independent investor.

But I don't want to minimize the potential risks in this game you're playing. You can limit the downside dangers, but the uncertainties in the equities market are still no illusion. There's little to cushion a loss. When you drop a bundle, you can't retrieve much of it through income tax write-offs. Given the current tax rules, for every dollar you lose you can only write off 50 cents up to the first $3,000. That's almost nothing.

Also, once you've lost a portion of your investing capital, it's extremely difficult to recoup. Unfortunately, your instinct then may be to take even greater risks to try to make it all back at once— you know, the old "double or nothing" syndrome.

In fact, 99.9 times out of 100, you will wind up losing all or almost all of your stake if you let this wild gambler's impulse take over. I've seen that happen time and time again.

Instead of such short-term, panic-based speculation, the wise investor will adopt the longer-term approach. Recovery from a bad loss will take some time, but you *will* recover if you keep a cool head and avoid digging an even deeper hole for yourself.

In line with the long-range approach, let me make a suggestion that at first glance may seem heretical: *Don't* keep a daily record of your portfolio. Look through it carefully on a monthly basis instead. This will help you avoid spur-of-the moment decisions.

In my early days I got carried away by the frenzy of one bull market and found myself making $5,000 in just one day even though I had a relatively modest portfolio. Because the market was soaring and I was leveraging my existing assets by buying on margin, I reaped a 20 percent return in just twenty-four hours.

It was fun keeping track of my growing fortune, and almost every time I had a free minute I'd recalculate my holdings. My daily record-keeping inspired me to invest larger and larger amounts on borrowed funds. I was truly caught up in the madness of the market, blinded by all my paper profits. Then came harsh reality. The market plunged, my margins were called, and the clout almost knocked me out of the market altogether. I'm sure that had I followed a more temperate program and checked my portfolio only occasionally, I wouldn't have been seduced into the destructive delirium that can be the undoing of so many market players.

Having attempted to explode the myths and shaky shibboleths related to common-stock investments, let me say that there is one frequently heard maxim that I do accept for the most part: "Sell on the good news and buy on the bad."

We've discussed this in some depth in earlier chapters, but I think it bears repeating here, in our discussion of common stocks, because it's precisely the opposite of what most novices feel they should do.

To understand the principle, look at it this way: Good news about a company has usually been "anticipated" by the market. That is, the stock has gone up as buyers have heard in advance about some positive future event. By the time there is a formal announcement from the corporation about its earnings or whatever, the stock has already hit the peak of its run. In fact, it's usually on its way back down when the news finally gets to you and you are in a position to buy. The smart investors have already started selling on the good news that has just been made public and, as a result, they are forcing the price of the common stock down.

Conversely, buying on bad news comes at a time when things are generally bleak. Unemployment is up, the market is down, and everyone is bad-mouthing the economy. This is an emotionally difficult time to buy. But you have an advantage if you move into the market at this point.

You see, as an individual investor, you have some time. You're not a professional trader who has to show relatively quick profits to impress a brokerage client or fund management. You can think in terms of a much longer-term commitment than the pros. And it's absolutely certain that if the stock market is in a valley, a relatively low point in one of its cycles, it will eventually go up again. You can wait for the upturn, whether it takes months, a year, or even longer, while the professionals can't. Take your time as the market moves through its broad cycles. Wait for equity prices to move lower, and then move in and find some bargains at that point.

By now a number of questions about buying and selling common stocks have probably popped into your mind. Let me throw out a few of the ones that I've been asked most frequently, and perhaps they will touch on some of the issues that bother you.

Question: Why do I always make the mistake of buying at the top and selling at the bottom?

As we've already seen, you are investing as an emotional person. The euphoria of the up markets gets to you. It is our experience that these markets always bring in the greatest number of new investors.

When everyone is talking about his or her market successes at cocktail parties, it becomes contagious. Everybody wants to get into the swim, and that includes you! Hence, the highest trading volume in the market usually comes near the peak in prices.

Conversely, it's a market tradition that low volume comes with lows in the prices. Of course, if people had more sense, they would be buying at the lows and selling at the highs. But the reality is precisely the opposite.

There is some mild consolation if you find yourself frequently getting into an emotional twit in your investing practice. You are not alone when you buy high and sell low. But it's scant comfort, isn't it, when you see your hard-earned money heading down the drain?

Question: Why do I always seem to miss out on maximizing my profits?

You can't possibly accumulate much if you trade out of securities too early, or if you trade too often. The general tendency, sadly, is to sell your winners too soon and to hang onto the losers forever.

You should do the reverse. Let your winners ride and ride and ride!

This is difficult, I acknowledge, because the pressure builds up as the paper profits increase. You become more and more fearful that your stock is going to peak out and start going down. There's an easy solution to this problem: Just *wait* for the downturn! If you're alert and you see what looks like a consistent downward trend getting under way, get on the phone and sell.

In using this approach you'll lose a little off what you would have made at the peak. But consider the alternative. If you sell too soon, the stock may not peak out until it has doubled again in value. Above all, remember one of those basic secrets of sound investing: You can't possibly sell precisely at the highest points and buy at the lowest points, at least not on a consistent basis; so don't even try.

With losing stocks there's another kind of destructive tendency. Most people tend to ride them down year in and year out, hoping against hope that they will come back to a magical price. It's as though there's a secret market number known to no one else in the world but you. The magic number, of course, is the price you paid for your dog, and a figure that has no connection at all with reality.

The best and the hardest advice I can give you is to identify these bad stocks after a limited period of time for what they are— losers. Then take your beating like an adult and walk away from them.

Question: How do you tell when a hot tip is really hot?

I have probably purchased fifty "hot tips" in my career, maybe even more. When I put them all together, I know I'm a net loser.

These "tips," perhaps well intended when they were secretly passed on to me, have usually been communicated by speculators. They may report that an important merger announcement is about to be made; or there may be information that a new product or a new service will be unveiled; or, perhaps, a dividend is about to be increased. Whatever they purport to report, they have one thing in common: The probability of your making a killing in them is infinitesimally low. You are far better off to ignore them and plod along more slowly, but more surely, toward long-term success.

Of course, I am resigned to the fact that the get-rich-quick fantasy is deep-seated in all of us, and it can be practically impossible to pass up a "sure thing." So, if you must, throw a small percentage of the invested capital you've set aside for speculation into these pipe dreams, which have lottery-size odds against your winning; but, by all means, *never* allow hot-tip investments to become a major ingredient of your portfolio strategy.

Question: When I buy a stock, should I put in a limit order or a market order?

My own experience is that once you have decided to buy or sell a security, you should put in a *market order*, which directs the broker to buy a certain amount of the stock at the best price that is next available on the exchange. Trying to engineer savings of ⅛ or ¼ of a point through a limit order, is plain silly. Witness my American Photocopy fiasco!

After all, if a stock is really worth buying, it's the big gains over the long haul that you're concerned about. The major moves in securities are the 50 percent and 100 percent moves over a period of a few months or perhaps a year in the great bull markets. So it's penny-wise and pound-foolish to chisel for the last ⅛ or ¼ of a point.

Question: Be honest, Chuck, can I really become my own stockbroker, or is this just a gimmick you're using to make this book more interesting?

Honest, you really *can* do it. How? Read this book; immerse yourself in the ebbs and flows of the investment world through proper reading and practical investment; and rely heavily on growth-oriented, no-load mutual funds.

Question: But to become really good at investing, doesn't it take an enormous amount of time?

You decide. It takes about a half hour a day to watch your investments and spend some time thinking about them. Then you take the time you would probably take anyhow for reading newspapers and articles relating to business and the markets. That's an extra hour or so.

That is some time, but it's not much; and it should be fun, not drudgery. More and more, as you get deeper into it, you will begin to find correlations between the stock market and other activities such as politics and international relationships and crises. To me, it's always been stimulating to keep informed of what is happening around the nation and the world. I think that makes anyone a more alert, interesting person.

Question: Is there any secret formula for a winning strategy with common stocks?

Yes, there is, but I wouldn't call it much of a secret. It consists of persistence, a long-term perspective, and personal discipline; and, of course, prudent diversification.

But let's be perfectly frank. In my candid opinion you will never get rich in the stock market in the sense that you will hit a jackpot. Except for the market geniuses and a few remarkably lucky individuals, that just is not possible.

On the other hand, good consistent returns in the 10 percent to 20 percent range over many years are not only possible, they are *probable* if you follow the guidelines that I've been laying out.

Question: But aren't there "systems" that will make you a winner more quickly if you just take time to learn about them?

Ahh, I have heard of so many systems that were supposed to lead me to that pot of gold at the end of the equity rainbow! Over the past quarter of a century I have pored through many books on "systems," and every last one of them has proved to have its own serious flaws.

Some are particularly gimmicky and demand an inordinate amount of time and technical analysis. They involve such arcane matters as "point and figure analysis" and "breakouts." There are also those strategies that involve buying or selling at special points indicated by certain mysterious, exotic signals on a special technical chart or computer graph.

These approaches are much too complicated for even above-average investors, and most of them have one particularly dangerous weakness: Their followers become so immersed in the system that they may miss the major moves in the market. And of what earthly use is that kind of system?

Much as I hate to dash the hopes of those who dream of some magic key to market success, I must say that in my experience over the years, I have found few investors, *very few,* who have been at all successful with any special system over a long period of time.

Question: What do you think of those investment advisers who predict gloom and doom for the stock market?

I'm definitely not of the gloom-and-doom school. The outlook I see for the rest of the decade is bright, not dark. We are safely out of the inflation-racked, shaky seventies, and Reaganomics seems to be working. Our economy has stabilized; we've got equilibrium in the financial markets with deregulation, and we have a classic long-term growth pattern evolving.

From time to time, no doubt, there will be "hiccups" in the markets. Some bear months will be interspersed with many more months of the bull. Overall I'm confident that we have created an extremely fine base for major growth for the remainder of the eighties. The financial markets are in good shape, and we can look to future technological advances to lead us forward and upward.

In my view there is a good climate afoot for long-term growth in common stocks, and the prospect of many opportunities for the alert independent investor. The outlook for bonds, however, is more of a mixed bag.

THE MIXED BAG OF BONDS

Many investors have been afflicted with an undue dose of caution, a result, I believe, of the frightening folk memories of the Great Depression. Older investors remember this period all too vividly from their own personal experience. Younger people have heard the awful stories from their elders about lost homes, ruined executives selling apples on street corners, and hotel clerks nonchalantly asking brokers as they registered, "Sleep or leap?"

From the investment point of view, we should put those sad old days into better perspective. The worst of the depression ran from the spectacular market crash in October 1929 until 1932. But even during those darkest days it wasn't straight down for the market. In the three-year period there were several giant rallies, a number of huge opportunities to make big money.

Still, misperception has persisted to this day, a fact that accounts, I suspect, for the undeserved popularity of bonds, those IOUs issued in return for fixed rates of interest by corporations and governments.

Should you buy them? My personal feeling is that you should not, though I'll mention a few exceptions to this sweeping generalization.

Bonds are primarily purchased for three reasons: first, for security; second, for relatively high yield in some stages of the economy; and last, in some cases for their tax exemption.

There is never going to be much of a reward over the long haul in buying high-quality bonds, because low risk means low yield. Even with high-quality issues, if you concentrate your financial eggs in one bond basket, you defeat the one real advantage in bonds—security. This is because, now and then, some bond-issuing companies do go out of business, and yours could be the one ready for trouble.

What you are looking for is quality, safety, and diversification. This goal can best be achieved not by relying on just one bond issue, but through a money market fund or a longer-term bond fund that might carry a hundred different bonds.

Bonds are an especially ridiculous proposition for investors in the first two life-cycle stages, stretching from their twenties to their middle years. These individuals can expect neither high income for the present nor high growth in the future.

For those approaching retirement and primarily interested in current income, individual bonds may offer a slightly better yield than some of the money market funds. But unless you choose very,

very wisely, you are back to square one, as far as security is concerned.

What it boils down to is this: For the older investor, there are few advantages in buying individual corporate bonds, though a bond fund may provide needed income for retirement. For the younger investor, there are even fewer advantages to buying individual bonds or shares in bond funds.

So that's my judgment on corporate bonds. But municipal bonds are another matter.

For your Aunt Nelly, who is rich and nervous, municipal bonds, issued by local governments, might be a good buy, especially since their interest payments are tax-exempt. But there's a major disadvantage in putting $25,000 into only one issue or type of these bonds. If you need to sell, there's a liquidity problem with such a small amount. Also, you have to compete against the professionals if you hope to get the best buys as they are offered on the various markets. You've got to have good connections and be quick, and most small investors are not in this position.

Another problem with municipals is that their yields may be only a mere 5 percent or so in a market where you can easily get 8 to 9 percent or higher with a money market fund or bank certificate of deposit. Thus, you must be in at least the 50 percent income tax bracket to derive any advantage from the tax-exempt feature.

If you insist on this highly conservative, no-growth, but safer type of investment, consider a mutual fund that specializes in tax-exempt bonds (i.e., unit investment trusts). That way you'll get diversification and you'll also have a big investment company making the purchases you might not be able to make by yourself.

The preceding was some of the "inside Schwab scoop" on stocks and bonds. Now let's take a look at a related topic, the highly dangerous, "gunslinging" option market. In particular, we'll discuss some of the finer points of puts and calls.

11

Some Fine Points on
Puts and Calls

IF you're new to the investment game, you may think that it's impractical for someone with limited experience to think about esoteric techniques like *puts* or *calls*. And you would be absolutely correct. Unless you employ these methods regularly, you may even forget what they are.

But after you've been around the investment scene a while, there's no reason for the terms to intimidate you. They're just options to buy or sell, and the basic concepts are really quite simple to grasp. Calls are an option to purchase a stock at a set price for a set time period. Those who buy calls are betting that the stock will go above a set price, and the difference in price will be their profit. To take advantage of diversification, I prefer to invest in one of the index options listed in the "S&P 100" column in your newspaper's financial pages. By investing this way you put your money into options on 100 major stocks, and not just one. In contrast, if you buy only one call, you have all your money riding on an option on one stock.

So, you might purchase a call, which gives you the right to buy 100 shares of stock at $20 for six months. If the stock goes up to $30 and you decide to exercise your option at that point, you'll realize a gain of $10 on each share of stock on which you bought the call.

CALL (STOCK) OPTION
Option to buy at a fixed (strike) price within a specified period.

Buyer/Holder	**Seller/Issuer/Writer**
Pays premium and commission.	Has to *sell* at agreed price if the option is exercised.
Guaranteed can *buy* stocks at a certain price.	
Betting market will rise above the strike price.	

PUT (STOCK) OPTION
Option to sell at a fixed (strike) price within a specified period.

Buyer/Holder	**Seller/Issuer/Writer**
Pays premium and commission.	Has to *buy* at agreed price if the option is exercised.
Guaranteed can *sell* stock at a certain price.	
Betting market will drop below the strike price.	

With puts, it's precisely the reverse. Here you are betting that the stock will drop in price. For example, you might purchase a put option on a certain stock at $10 a share. If the stock drops to $5, you can still sell the put option at a profit.

Today, most put and call options are traded on the American Stock Exchange in New York, the Chicago Board of Options Exchange, the Philadelphia Stock Exchange, and the Pacific Exchange. These listed options are the most popular for most investors. As I've already said, I think the best approach for any investor interested in options is to buy one of the index options.

These are listed regularly in the daily paper and provide diversification.

Years ago there were only over-the-counter options, and those are still available today. But the most popular are those listed on the exchanges given above. The period covered by the options ranges from one day to nine months, after which they expire.

If you are holding a call option that expires in ten days, and the stock does not rise within that ten-day time frame, you lose your investment when the option expires. Similarly, with a put option that lasts for, say, two months until expiration, you lose your investment unless the stock decreases below the exercise price during that two-month period.

The first three or four years that options reached general popularity, the newspaper financial sections carried only the quotations for calls on various securities. But now puts are listed as well.

Personally, I'm not enthusiastic about puts and calls unless a person has (1) gone through at least one complete market cycle as an active investor and (2) has had some experience with no-load mutual funds. I consider them a short-term approach to investing, and since I advocate mostly long-term techniques to build up a solid asset base, these options have a limited value for me.

There are some advantages to options that can fit into a long-term investment philosophy. With calls, for example, you can enjoy some extra income on some individual stocks you own, if you're willing to risk the fact that they may be called away from you in a rising market.

Take the best case: You may sell a call option on a blue chip stock you intend to hold and pocket a few hundred dollars from the premium you receive. Then, if the stock goes down, stays the same, or moves up only slightly (less than enough to cover any broker's commission for handling a transaction), your shares won't be "called" (i.e., bought through the exercise of the option) away from you. Instead, you'll not only get to keep the stock and any dividends that may be declared on it, but you'll also have the premium that was paid for the option to provide an extra boost to your income.

But there's the other side of the option-writing coin: If the stock you own really soars and you've sold a call option on it, you just have to sit tight, grit your teeth, and watch the holder of the option ride the profits upward. You will have the premium you've been paid and a modest appreciation on your original price, up to the *strike, or striking, price* of the option (or the price at which you have agreed to sell it). But that may be small consolation if you happen to have sold your option at the beginning of a major bull market.

Some people are great advocates of puts and calls as a way to increase dramatically the size of their portfolios in short periods of time. I'm wary of this investment philosophy. In order to make a profit you have to be very expert or very lucky to be right more often than not over periods of just a few months. That's quite a difficult trick to perform. But there are plenty of people who don't share my pessimism.

A few investors go so far as to place the major portion of their portfolios into high-yield, low-risk investments, e.g., Treasury bills. Then they take the remaining 10 to 20 percent of their holdings to play calls—especially the general market option indices like the "S&P 100."

To illustrate, say an investor has $20,000 worth of capital. Of that, 95 percent, or $19,000, goes into a money market fund and the other 5 percent, or $1,000, is placed in calls on the "S&P 100." If the market moves up handsomely, he or she will enjoy a nice profit on that $1,000 investment. But even if the market goes down, all is not lost, because the bulk of the person's investment remains in conservative holdings.

Playing options this way purely as speculation does involve a minimal amount of money. But so does playing blackjack. The key is to discipline yourself so that you have a definite, relatively low ceiling on the money you're willing to risk. When that is gone, you must quit. Otherwise, you may lose all you have before you even know what's happened. You see, playing options places a great premium not only on good judgment about a stock, but also on *timing*. You may be exactly right about the potential for a stock, but if you take out a ninety-day option, which is based on a completely correct anticipation of the market, you will still lose if it

takes the stock ninety-*one* days to behave in the way you anticipated.

Frankly, I've seen more abuse in options by the regular brokerage houses than in any other form of investment. One reason
for the temptation to lure investors into options is that the commissions can be rolled up to an incredibly high level before the
unwary investor even knows what has happened.

For example, if you were to buy one option to purchase 100
shares of stock, the commission would be the same as for buying
100 shares of that stock. Obviously, you can afford to buy many
more options than you can 100-lot shares. So the broker has an
overwhelming incentive to lure you into option playing—and in
recent years I've seen more people lose money quickly through
options than through any other form of investment. The byword
for options, then, is: Tread lightly!

One friend of mine is a fellow weekend athlete, a very bright
guy formerly with a prestigious New York company. In a mere
six months his brokers took his hard-earned capital and lost a great
deal of it. Needless to say, he quit using these brokers. The only
consolation—for the brokers, that is, not for my friend—was that
they wound up with $10,000 worth of commissions for their firm.

The moral to this story is: Until you have devoted a good
amount of time to getting market experience, I'd advise that you
return to the "Monopoly" board. Play this hazardous field in *sim-
ulated* fashion through at least one bull and one bear cycle, without risking real money. Then, when you are sure about what you're
doing, you may want to gamble a little. But if you do start playing
options for keeps, don't ever spend more than 5 percent of your
investment portfolio on them, or 10 percent at the very most.

In our own Schwab company, about 20 percent of our commissions come from buying and selling options, and of course we're
glad to get the money. By our company policies, I can't give advice directly to any of our customers who pursue this form of investment. But here I can say to you investors who are into puts
and calls that we're happy to handle your business, and we'll do
it at the lowest possible cost. But be careful. *Please* follow the advice outlined in this book, and take it easy!

For my own portfolio, I go even farther. These days I won't touch any options except occasional forays into the index options. Why? Because I've never had much luck with them and the various strategies connected with them don't apply any more to my personal portfolio.

But if I know you, you'll want to find out on your own whether they're your kind of investment. So below are some common questions that I hear about options, with my answers, to round out your preliminary education. If you're going to try options, I at least want you to be well prepared and in a position to protect yourself as much as possible. First, we'll consider questions about call options, and then we'll turn to puts.

Question: Why buy call options at all?

You have a great deal of leverage on your money when you buy an option. The reason is that you have to pay much less for the option than for the underlying stock; yet you have the potential for making as much on an option as on the stock itself *if* the price of the stock (and the value of the option) increases. So there is an opportunity to make a fat profit on a small investment. Also, you know the full extent of your risk. You cannot lose more than the price of the option, plus the commission you paid on it.

Question: What are the objections to buying options?

Options are classified as "wasting assets." That is, they become totally worthless if you have taken no action on them by their expiration day. The necessary action is to buy the underlying stock if you hold a call option, or to sell if you have a put option. Also, if the underlying stock has appreciated in price for a call (or depreciated for a put), you could sell the call or put option itself for a nice profit before it expires, without touching the underlying stock.

By contrast, a stock that you hold may depreciate in value. But there is always *some* value in it, unless the company goes bankrupt.

Question: How do I get into option trading?

If you want to be conservative and you can use the extra income, you may "write," or sell, call options on stocks you own. Your broker will arrange this transaction for you. Or your broker can arrange for you to buy or sell any put or call option.

Remember: Investors who write calls do not expect the price of the underlying stock to rise above the strike price. They tend to be bears. The buyers of calls, on the other hand, are more bullish and do expect the price of the underlying stock to rise above the strike price. Conversely, those who write puts expect that the stock price will rise above the strike, or exercise price. They are bulls.

Question: Suppose that during the life of the option I change my mind?

You can simply sell your option contract at the going market price.

Question: But suppose the other fellow in the transaction objects?

It is all handled through the Options Clearing Board. There is always a buyer for every seller, but each transaction is executed anonymously.

Question: What is the premium?

This is the money paid by the option buyer to the seller, whether it is a put or a call. The seller keeps this money, but it does *not* represent a down payment toward purchase of the underlying stock. It is the risk that the buyer undertakes and becomes a no-strings-attached profit for the seller.

Question: Are there trades in premiums?

Yes. Many buyers aren't interested in consummating the option contract. Instead, they gamble that they will later be able to unload the contract at a higher premium price than they paid for it.

Question: Can you give an example of the underlying factors that go into the determination of premium prices?

A major one is the length of the option. A higher price will be attached to one that extends the maximum nine-month period set by a given exchange because it gives the investor a longer run for his money, during which the market may turn to his advantage. Also, if a stock is generally regarded as a "hot" prospect, likely to go up in the near future, the cost of the call option will tend to be higher.

Question: Does the state of the market itself influence premium prices?

In bull markets, investors want to buy call options, but those who own securities are less inclined to write them. Hence, premium prices go up. In bear markets, the opposite holds. An added factor is the character of the underlying stock. If the stock is given to wide fluctuations in a particular market, the premium is usually higher than for a narrow-moving stock.

Question: Are options similar to stocks?

Yes, in many ways. They are traded on certain exchanges, and the buy and sell orders are executed by brokers just as they would exercise stock orders to buy or sell. Like stocks, the option prices are reported daily in many major newspapers.

Question: Are there any major differences between options and stocks?

With stocks, there are a limited number of shares. But there are as many options as there are buyers and sellers for them. The trading in options merely involves printed statements from the brokerage houses, which minimizes delay in consummating the transactions. With stocks, on the other hand, official certificates are required.

Question: Does option trading offer flexibility?

Yes, great flexibility. You might possess options on one kind of stock that all expire on the same day. But the options may have different striking prices, or exercise prices, because they were bought at different times. Or you may obtain options with varying expiration dates, to give yourself a little more leeway in case you misjudge the movement of a market cycle.

Question: If you can, give an example of an option's superiority over a stock.

The owner of a stock may lose much more than the buyer of a call option because the amount of loss of the option buyer is fixed and limited to the premium. The stock owner, on the other hand, can't predict the precise amount of his possible loss in the throes of a bear market. In addition, an option buyer has more leverage for his money because he can control more stock for less money than the person who actually pays "up front" for a block of stock.

Question: How can options help the conservative investor?

It's possible to protect yourself against a down movement in the market and at the same give yourself the opportunity to enjoy an upward movement. The strategy depends on buying both puts and calls, and also sometimes on writing call options on underlying stock you hold. But this takes a great deal of careful analysis and many precise calculations. Don't get into this ploy unless you are willing to take time to figure out exactly how it can work successfully in the current market, in light of your own personal investment objectives.

Question: I've heard some people say in regard to options, "You can have your cake and eat it too." What do they mean?

Maybe something like this: Instead of purchasing shares of stock, you might buy calls on the same number. Then you put the remainder of your money into short-term, interest-bearing bonds or money market funds. The interest sharply cuts the cost of the calls, while the calls themselves offer you a chance to profit in a rising market.

There's also another form of "cake eating." Suppose you want to buy stock X, but you can't afford it at the moment. By purchasing a call, you limit the maximum price you will have to pay for the stock, maybe as far in the future as nine months later.

Question: I have only a modest sum to invest in the market—too modest, I'm afraid, to obtain diversification. Can calls help me?

Instead of buying a single stock with a modest sum such as $5,000, some people spread the risk by buying several calls in different companies or by buying one of the market index options. But caution! If your total stake is $5,000, *don't* put all of it into calls. Never do that! Most, if not all, of the small investor's money should go into no-load mutual funds.

Question: I've heard the phrases "in-the-money" call and "out-of-the-money" call. What do they mean?

When the current market value of the stock is above the exercise, or striking, price it is an *in-the-money* call. When the market price is below the strike price, it is an *out-of-the-money* call. In-the-money options always command higher premiums.

Question: What exactly is the procedure in writing a call?
It's simple. Here are the steps:

Step 1: Determine through the published quotations the price of the premium you are willing to accept and the duration of the call that you are willing to write.

Step 2: Deposit your stock with your broker and tell him to sell the call option at the "market price" or "limit premium" price. A limit premium price is one which you specify, rather than just any price that happens to prevail when the broker goes out to sell your call.

Step 3: He will credit your account with the amount of the premium, less commission. In almost all cases, you will keep any cash dividends on the underlying stock until the option is called by the buyer at the strike price.

Question: What is a covered call?
This is a situation where you own the stock, or perhaps the convertible bonds or preferreds or warrants, that stand behind the call.

Question: What do you think about writing a "naked" call option?
Writing a "naked," or uncovered, option means writing one against stock you don't actually own. It's issued against your cash deposit, rather than any underlying security, and involves a form of playing the market on margin. The investor must have funds on margin with his broker to make certain he will be able to purchase and deliver the stock if the call is made.

This is dangerous business. I can add nothing to the following cautionary note by the Chicago Board Options Exchange: "Uncovered calls should . . . be written only by individuals who fully understand the substantial risks and are willing and financially able to assume them."

Unlike an ordinary option, in which your loss is limited to the premium you have paid, the writing of a "naked" call option means you must actually buy and deliver the stock. In a sharply rising market you could suffer heavy losses with this strategy. Not recommended!

Question: Can writing covered call options ever serve as a hedge against loss?

Very much so. The amount of the premium, less commission, will offset to a certain extent any price drop in your underlying stock. For the wary investor, this may be a good strategy. Of course, if you do this in a rising market, you'll limit your gains to any upward movement of the stock to the strike price, plus the premium.

Question: How does "variable hedging" come into the picture?

This is a tricky maneuver involving the writing of a covered option, plus one or more "naked" options. In a down market the investor can realize a sizable profit. But the "naked" options pose a considerable risk. Again, I don't recommend this, except perhaps for those who have a lot of experience in the market and are willing to shoulder heavy losses, if necessary.

Question: How do I decide what calls to write?

I can only give a thumbnail sketch of the factors you should take into consideration. The decision will be up to you based on a more detailed analysis of your individual needs and the current opportunities in the market.

First of all, determine whether you are presently bearish or bullish on market conditions. Your attitude will influence the striking price you want, the length of the option you prefer, and your relative willingness to have the stock called away from you.

With a low striking price, you will enjoy a fatter premium and more protection in the event of a market slide. With a high striking price, you forego a fat premium but ensure greater profit if the stock does indeed move upward.

Having covered some of main questions that may pop into your mind about call options, let's talk about puts.

First of all, remember the basic definition: When you are buying a put, you are getting the right to sell at a predetermined price within a specified period. It's the precise opposite of a call option.

For speculation, the put is much preferable to selling a stock short. Short sellers must pay a considerably higher commission and then resign themselves to potentially limitless risk and margin calls. They may even incur the responsibility for dividend payment. By contrast, the put buyer not only carries a known, limited risk, but also has the leverage that will maximize his potential profits.

Put buyers can also afford to be much braver than short sellers. For example, a stock may suddenly spurt upward, and then decline. The short seller is often seriously tempted to cover his short sale at a loss, rather than wait for the decline that would have brought him a profit. With much less at risk, the put buyer can wait for the decline (at least until the expiration date).

Now, for a few pertinent questions.

Question: When should I execute a put?

If the underlying stock sags considerably below the original agreed-on strike price, the put owner may profit by selling his rights. Or he may decide to claim his right to "put," or deliver, the stock at the original contract price. He then delivers stock he already owns; or he buys it in the market at a depressed price and "puts" it at the original, higher price.

By and large, because of the considerably lower commission,

most investors prefer selling the put rather than delivering the stock.

Question: How can puts serve as insurance?

Let's say you own stock that you expect will drop in price, but you don't want to unload it. Perhaps, if you bought it well below its present value, you don't want to incur the sizable tax that would result from sale now at a profit. In such a case, puts would serve as a cushion against a possible market drop.

Question: How do puts serve as hedges?

If you are invested totally in speculative stocks—a practice I do *not* recommend except for a modest share of your portfolio— puts can be extremely valuable as a hedge. Hedging involves making two opposite-direction investments so that your risk is minimized.

Here's a way you might employ puts to do some hedging: The same day you take a flyer in a speculative issue, you buy a put with the same striking price as the price you pay for the stock itself. In this way you can only lose the amount of the premium if the stock skids disastrously. If, on the other hand, the stock really soars, the lost premium is a trifling expense compared to your profits. If none of your investments moves up or down, your put becomes worthless. Then, if you want to renew this form of "investment insurance," you'll have to buy another put.

Question: How can puts help me diversify my portfolio?

The same way that calls can. Instead of tying up funds to sell short on the stock of company A, you can spread your money— and your risk—by acquiring puts in companies A, B, and C. But keep in mind that you should regard this as diversification of your *speculative* investments only. Don't make the mistake of putting too much of your money here.

Question: I expect there will be a major movement in the price of some of my stock, but I don't know whether it will be up or down. Can puts or calls help me?

The answer is they may help through a *straddle*, but the extent to which this technique will help remains to be seen. A straddle involves buying both a put and a call with the same striking price and expiration date on the same shares of stock. The only difference between the two investments is that you will probably pay different premium prices for the put and call.

This is another eat-your-cake-and-have-it-too strategy. You get a chance to chalk up a profit; at the same time, you are given considerable protection. If the stock moves either up or down more than the combined premium costs of the put and call, you are assured a profit. Only if the stock remains on dead center in its price, do you sacrifice the total amount of the premiums.

Of course, there is one factor that takes a bit of the bloom off this seemingly no-lose rose: Trading in more than one option means paying more than one commission.

Question: To keep proper perspective, what questions should I always ask myself in buying puts?

Do I want to buy a put with a long or short duration? Do I prefer in-the-money, at-the-money, or out-of-the-money puts? How do I feel about the underlying stock? Am I motivated by a desire for protection or for speculative profit?

Now, for a few final warnings and tips on puts:

• Understand that as a seller of a put you must keep enough funds with your broker to make sure you can buy the stock if the put is exercised. And you must realize that the buyer of the put *may* demand to excercise the put of the stock at any point before the expiration date. Also, he most assuredly *will* demand it when the market price drops markedly below the striking price. But like the call seller, the put seller can limit his loss potential by purchasing a similar put at the current market price and close out his position.

- Never write (issue) a put on a stock that you wouldn't want to own at the striking price, less the premium.
- A higher exercise price means a larger premium—and also increases the chance that the put will be exercised.
- Don't buy a put against a stock and also sell the stock short. This is a superbearish strategy that only market-wise investors, who arc willing to accept a major risk, can afford to undertake.

There are many other variations for puts and calls than we've discussed here. In fact, there are so many that the Chicago Board Options Exchange has put together a number of booklets, some of which you might like to study. They include:

Understanding Options: A Guide to Puts and Calls
Are Call Options for You?
Are Put Options for You?
Buying Puts, Straddles and Combinations
Call Option Writing Strategies
Tax Considerations in Using CBOE Options
Understanding GNMA Options
Understanding Treasury Bond Options
Writing Puts, Straddles and Combinations

These are available through a discount brokerage house like ours or through a full-commission broker. Or you may obtain them from CBOE, LaSalle at Jackson, Room 2200, Chicago, IL 60604. For a prospectus on the work of the Options Clearing Corporation, write CBOE; or write the Clearing Corporation itself at 200 S. Wacker Drive, 27th floor, Chicago, IL 60606.

Reading these publications is, of course, optional. But there are three other publications that you *must* study before you embark on this fascinating but risky form of investment:

Before buying or selling an option, your broker must give you

Understanding the Risks and Uses of Listed Options. You should also get *The S & P 100 Index: The Option Edge* to learn more about the use of market indices in buying puts and calls.

As you can see, the powers that be do not take option trading lightly. Neither should you. With the added leverage options give you, the profit potential becomes much higher than with buying stocks; but when you lose, you can lose big and quickly.

12

Making Sense Out of the Mutual Fund Maze

On a number of occasions I've mentioned in general terms the advantage of owning a mutual fund. In this chapter I get more specific.

A mutual fund, you'll recall, is an investment company which holds stock in many individual corporations and sells its own shares to the general public. Consequently, if you hold just one share in a mutual fund, you have a little "piece," through the fund's holdings, of many other corporations. A mutual fund thus offers automatic diversification to the investor.

Mutual funds come in two main types, *load* and *no-load*. The load funds typically charge 8½ percent commissions and are sold through full-comission brokerage houses. Funds also charge a yearly management fee that is deducted from the holdings of the shareholders. The no-loads, in contrast, charge no commission, though they do have yearly management fees.

I only recommend no-load funds. In fact, I think anyone who chooses a load over a no-load fund is seriously uninformed at best, and insane at worst. I will concentrate almost entirely in this chapter on the benefits and uses of the no-load company. Here are some of the advantages of no-loads:

- *Expert selection of securities.* Experts in the particular field in which the fund concentrates, which may be anything from energy to electronics, choose the portfolio. That puts them in a better position than you or I will ever be in to evaluate a group of stocks.
- *Professional management.* There is constant surveillance and management of these funds by pros who devote all their time and expertise to their group of stocks. They add regularly to their holdings, cull bad issues, and do their best to run their back offices, or record-keeping departments, efficiently. Of course, a well-run firm with an excellent performance record will mean a greater influx of investors' money and, hence, more management fees to reward good management.
- *Diversification.* No-load mutual funds may comprise anywhere from twenty-five or thirty securities to more than one hundred. So if one issue within a portfolio goes sour, the overall impact for fund shareholders is minimal.
- *No high sales charges.* Because the old-fashioned load funds carry sales charges as high as 8½ percent, you have to earn that on your investment before you even begin to realize a gain. In other words, if you invest $10,000, $850 of your hard-earned money immediately gets taken out as a commission. That means you really start out with an investment of $9,150, and the fund managers have to cause your shares to appreciate up to $10,000 again before you just break even.

    In contrast, no-load funds have no sales charges. There are also some *low-load* funds that carry only nominal commissions, and you may want to consider these as well.
- *Low fees.* Annual no-load fund management fees are quite competitive and reasonable, usually in the range of ½ of 1 percent.
- *Security selections tailored to your special interests.* Whatever your investment desires, there is probably a fund that concentrates in that area. A sampling of possibilities includes

funds that specialize in energy, gold- and silver-mining companies, tax-free income, long-term bonds, foreign securities, high-growth companies, high-technology companies, government securities, oil and gas, and a dozen or more other specific fields.

• *An investment philosophy for everybody.* If you are young and aggressive or older and more conservative, you can find a fund that matches your objectives. You can invest in funds that are income-oriented, growth-oriented, or a combination of these factors.

These are some of the attractions that have made me a no-load funds enthusiast for some twenty years. But how do you pick out a good fund, one that is likely to appreciate significantly in price over the next few years?

The trick is to track the performance of any fund that interests you over a fairly long period of time, at least five years, and preferably ten or more. Check how well the managers are doing, and be certain that if a fund is a good performer, the current managers were in the driver's seat in previous successful years.

I recommend the following procedure to check out your fund prospects.

Step 1: Study for a little while the daily performance of your chosen fund or funds. Most major newspapers publish the prices in special columns on the financial pages.

When you locate the mutual fund listings, you will find two figures for each fund, the net asset value and what you must pay to buy into it. If the numbers on the left and the right sides are identical, that's a no-load fund. But if one number is, say, $9.15 and the other is $10, that means you're looking at a load fund, that is, you have to pay $10 to buy one share of a fund worth $9.15. The difference in price, 85 cents, is the 8½ percent commission you're going to be charged.

In addition, *The Wall Street Journal* often carries articles on mutual funds, and *Barron's* and *Forbes* magazines periodically publish mutual fund ratings. *Money* is another good source of information.

Step 2: To delve more deeply into the background of a fund, as far back as, say, twenty years, consult the *Weisenberger Report*. This annual publication is available in business libraries.

Step 3: By all means, write to your candidate fund for a prospectus. By law, all funds must provide detailed information about their objectives and disclose any other pertinent information.

An important consideration at this stage is whether your fund belongs to a "family" of funds. It's often advantageous to buy a fund related to several others, usually through the same management. In this case, you may be able to move your money back and forth among the various members of the "family" without incurring certain fees or going through the complicated and time-consuming process of selling and buying from scratch.

Step 4: If you desire to dig even deeper into the no-loads, there are other annuals and magazines, as well as books, that can help you. For this information, write to the No-Load Mutual Fund Association, 11 Penn Plaza, Suite 2204, New York, NY 10001.

Step 5: Finally, you may want to subscribe to a newsletter that covers no-load mutuals. I can suggest four offhand, though I don't want this list to be construed as a recommendation:

Donoghue's MoneyLetter, Box 411, Holliston, MA 01746

No-Load Fund X, DAL Investment Company, 235 Montgomery St., San Francisco, CA 94104

The No-Load Fund Investor, P.O. Box 283, Hastings-on-Hudson, NY 10706

Guide to Worry-Free Investing, Wellington Financial Corp., 1800 Grosvenor Center/733 Bishop St., Honolulu, HI 96813

After you've taken these preliminary steps, you need to consider a few other factors before you make a choice. All other things being equal, you may want to go with a small mutual fund than a large one. A major reason is that a billion-dollar fund will probably not have the potential to move up as fast as one carrying only $20 to $30 million in investments.

The smaller funds, enjoying much more flexibility, can take highly meaningful positions in smaller companies. If they put their money into a few new ventures and those ventures take off, the fund's shareholders will also find the value of their shares moving up rather rapidly. The billion-dollar funds, in contrast, are a bit muscle-bound; their holdings are too massive for any one stock or a few holdings to make that much difference.

But it's the old "R & R" story, risk and reward. There is more risk in the smaller funds because if their management guesses wrongly, their losses will be proportionately greater. Even one bad investment can be felt by the fund's shareholders.

This is fairly easy to understand. Suppose your fund invests in only 30 securities, and one of them is a disaster. That one bad egg represents 3⅓ percent of the total portfolio. On the other hand, in a fund containing 300 companies in its portfolio, one stock represents a mere ³⁄₁₀ of 1 percent. So the impact there is minimal.

Fortunately, rules restrict the funds from overinvestment in any one security. The most that can be put into a single security is 5 percent of the fund, and one fund is allowed to invest in no more than 10 percent of the stock of any company. These are excellent precautions, especially for the more aggressive funds whose volatility might otherwise get out of hand and whose influence on any one stock could be unhealthy.

But even with these limitations you can still get quite a ride out of an aggressive, growth-oriented mutual fund. The potential action is related to what financiers call their "high beta." The fund's reaction to up markets and down markets greatly outpaces the market itself.

For example, when the market goes up 10 percent, the fund may soar 30 percent. On the other hand, if the market drops 10 percent, the fund could easily exhibit three times that volatility and skid down 30 percent.

Hence, even for those of you in the twenty-five to thirty-five age bracket, I recommend that no more than 50 percent of your total investment portfolio be put into a highly aggressive, "gunslinging" mutual fund. The other half should go into a fund geared to more conservative growth.

For the higher-age brackets, I recommend an even more cautious approach to the "gunslingers." But for all of the funds, if you can afford it, I suggest that the dividends and capital gains be reinvested. In that way you will enjoy an extra, highly desirable compounding effect.

Let's turn our attention to the practicalities of buying a no-load mutual fund. First of all, imagine that you walk "cold turkey" into a full-commission stock brokerage firm, *any* of the major firms, and ask to see someone about buying a no-load. They may not laugh at you; they may not even show you the door; but they won't sell you a no-load fund. After all, full-commission brokers have to earn a living too, even if it's at your expense!

Now, they may offer to help you *liquidate* any no-load fund you hold. But, almost certainly, they will immediately invite you to buy into a full-load fund. They'll make some arguments about how much better the fund they are pushing is than various no-loads. For example, they may point out that their load fund has had a better growth rate than such-and-such no-load fund.

But don't get hoodwinked. Sure, there are load funds that have performed better than no-loads. But there are also many no-loads that have done better than loads. In the last analysis, which is better, a good no-load or a good load? If you don't know the answer to this by now, turn back to the beginning of this chapter and start again.

How, exactly, do you go about buying a no-load fund if you can't do it through a regular full-commission broker? I must admit that the traditional way of buying no-loads is cumbersome and time-consuming. You have to go through the following stately maneuvers:

- After deciding on the fund that appeals to you, you write or call its office for the prospectus and application form. This will take a few days.
- After filling out the form, you return it with your check to the fund office. Add another two or three days for this procedure.
- On the day your application is received, it will be processed for issuance of the shares the following business day, at that day's net asset value.

- Finally, you will receive notification in the mails that the shares have been purchased in your name.

Now, what if you want to redeem or sell your shares? You then have to go through this slow minuet:

- You mail them in a letter, with your signature guaranteed by a bank or stock exchange member firm. The letter should say something like, "I am redeeming my shares. Please remit the funds to me."
- Depending on the mails, you will receive your check in from seven days to two weeks.

But there's another way. You may be able to find a discount broker who will handle the transaction for you and enable you to cut out considerable hassle and wasting of time in the process. Here's the way it works, step by step:

Step 1: You may have your choice of more than two hundred no-load and low-load funds, ranging from aggressive growth funds to income funds to tax-exempt funds.

Step 2: With just one phone call to a discount broker's mutual fund trading department, you put in your buy or sell order.

Step 3: The order is executed at the next closing price of the fund on the same day you call (provided you call during hours when the market is open for trading).

Step 4: The day after the transaction, confirmation should be mailed to you. It will show the number of shares and the dollar amount in the transaction, plus the fee you have paid. The fee for such a transaction at one such discount company is one-third lower than the regular discount brokerage commission schedule, so it really pays to choose the no-load mutual fund route.

To reverse the process, you can sell your fund shares through just one phone call. This makes your fund investment as liquid as an investment in individual stocks.

It's also possible, in some cases, to buy mutual funds on margin. The possibility of using margin with your funds means you can borrow against your stake in the fund for other purposes, such as buying a car or paying college bills for your children. Your investment in these funds, by the way, should be protected by the broker like any of your other securities—through the Securities Investor Protection Corporation (SIPC) and perhaps private insurance companies as well.

Finally, I would strongly recommend that you take advantage of one of the major conveniences of mutual fund investing: the ability to add regular, fixed, relatively low dollar amounts to your holdings. For example, unlike ordinary stock investing, you might add $100 per month or quarter to your chosen fund without the higher commissions that would be charged for odd-lot stock investing. This technique will also make it easy to take advantage of the principle of dollar-cost averaging (i.e., adding regular amounts to equity holdings at fixed intervals to take advantage of the overall upward movement of the stock market).

Before we leave this discussion of mutual funds, let me offer three caveats about buying them.

Caveat 1: The first, which applies to the purchase of any security, is that most assessments of a fund or a company must be largely historical in that they are based on past performance. In all the literature you will find, tucked away somewhere, a phrase that says, in effect, "There are no guarantees about the future." So true, so true!

All that past history can do is give you some inkling about the style of the management, their capability, and the strength of their organization.

Caveat 2: Even though your mutual fund will be broad based, I would still urge you to spread your risk by buying several funds— and "several" means *not* all in the same family of funds. The problem is that you can never tell about what may happen to the management of an organization.

For example, the key men may all be reaching retirement age at about the same time. In that case, you can only hope they will leave competent managers behind. Or a fund may have a great track record and then find itself deeply involved with the wrong securities just because of bad judgment.

So, once again I say, "Diversify!"

Caveat 3: The more successful you are with your fund buys or other securities, the more you have to plan ahead for the tax consequences. Unless you arrange for a separate cash flow to cover the taxes on your capital gains and dividends, you may get caught short. You could find you'll have to dump your winners at whatever price you can get, regardless of the state of the market, to pay the piper when April 15 rolls around.

But having sounded these warnings, let me leave you with this more positive thought: On balance, a good no-load mutual fund—and there are many of them—is about the best investment you can make. It has everything, and every wise investor should have substantial holdings in two or three no-load funds in his or her portfolio.

13

A Guide to "Parking" Cash
in the Money Market Lot

EVERY SO OFTEN, between making investments in the market, you may want to take a break, step back, and mull over the situation. It's not always easy to make one important decision after another. For example, sometimes it takes time to decide what to buy if you've just spent long, agonizing days trying to determine whether or not to sell.

Certainly, it's important to take whatever time is necessary to exercise good judgment in a situation like this. But, at the same time, you want your cash to be working for you. In other words, you need a liquid place to "park" your money at a high interest rate while you make up your mind.

But where to go? A money market fund? A bank savings account? A checking account? All have that precious quality of liquidity which you want most of all. But how do they differ in comparative safety and yield?

Let's talk for a moment about the money market funds, because they have been riding a wave of popularity in recent years. Money market funds arose in the first place out of an aberration in our economic history. I'm referring to the tremendous inflation we had back in the 1970s.

Bank and savings institutions were at a disadvantage with their savings accounts because they could offer only 5 or 5¼ percent interest on totally liquid deposits. On their CDs (certificates of deposit) they could pay 9 percent, 10 percent, even upward of 20 percent at one point. But at that time CDs were available only in amounts of $100,000 or higher. That effectively blocked the little fellow from getting a piece of the high interest rates available.

Enter the money market funds to fill this void. They accepted deposits in dribs and drabs of $20,000, $10,000, $5,000, and soon even smaller amounts. Then, when they had raised $100,000, the funds purchased bank CDs at the high interest rates and allowed the small investor to share in the bounty.

The managers of these firms were smart enough to invest in government securities, which are about as safe as you can get, and in CDs and bankers' acceptances, which are somewhat less safe, but still safe enough for me. Also, they got into short-term money market instruments that carry little or no risk.

Every such fund is market-valued every day on the basis of the value of the paper it holds. For most funds, the average maturity in their portfolios is between twenty and forty days. The longer the term on a note or bond bought by the fund, the higher the yield. Conversely, so long as the yield curves are in normal position, the short-term money market instruments pay the lowest rates.

Between 1977 and 1982, when money market funds were raking in the cash, the situation for individuals as well as for banks was ridiculous. The small investor could get a decent market rate of interest only by withdrawing his or her funds from the bank and joining a money market fund. The fund then, in effect, deposited the individual's money right back into the bank by purchasing CDs!

In a cockeyed sort of way, the banks were thus competing with themselves. They lost savings account money they had secured at 5 percent, only to end up paying an exorbitant 18 percent when they issued the CDs.

In this period of high and rising rates, the money market funds ballooned from almost nothing to well in excess of $200 billion. Then, in December 1982 and January 1983, there was a watershed decision that deregulated the banks and allowed them to pay a market rate of interest on certain accounts of $2,500 or more.

With this competition from deregulated banks, the money market funds capped out at about $240 billion, and in a year they lost some $60 billion in deposits. It's possible that from now on their competitive advantage will be zilch, but so volatile and unpredictable is the money market these days that you just never know.

Wherever you decide to park your money, you should keep an eagle eye on your rates. But if you can get the same rate from your bank as from a fund, you are, in my opinion, better off with the bank because there you have full checking privileges and FDIC insurance up to $100,000.

To be perfectly frank, I no longer see any clear advantage in the money market funds. The banks are now free to set whatever rates they want, and as soon as loan demand strengthens, they will have great flexibility in attracting money from the money market funds.

After all, the funds merely take your money and put it into CDs or government securities. Then they charge an override of, let's say, between ½ and 1 percent for the service (fees plus administrative costs).

I don't say they'll become dinosaurs, as I expect will happen with the load mutual funds. No, money market funds will be around in some size and importance in the years ahead. But it's hard for me to see any clear, long-term competitive advantage that they have. I'll admit that I park some of my cash in money market positions, just to satisfy the need to diversify, but I look first to my banks, which usually offer a competitive rate and also provide conveniences like complete check-writing privileges and cash machines.

Also, don't forget this important fact about your bank: If you ever need to borrow money, it's better to have a strong banking relationship, because money market funds aren't going to lend you any money. If you plan to buy a house or a car, let your friendly neighborhood bank know you love it with a substantial savings deposit.

Now, let's field a few questions.

Question: You downplay the future role of the money market funds, but do you mean to say that banks are the wave of the future for "parking" our cash?

Yes, and they always have been. Banks have now been given the opportunity to compete, and that means, I think, they will be unbeatable in fulfilling this "cash-parking" function. Banks have many advantages over money market funds, and I've already described many of them. But I believe that ten years from now the funds will still be competing, though they will continue to decline after their 1982 peak.

Question: Instead of using a bank, isn't there something to be said for using a "family" of funds, where you can move easily back and forth from a growth mutual fund to a money market fund?

At first glance, this "family of funds" arrangement may seem superior to using a bank, which requires you to take out your money before you send it off to a fund. But there are other ways to achieve the same end. For example, certain discount brokerage firms will automatically sweep your money into a money market fund or into a bank if that money is sitting around uninvested.

Question: Some have argued that you can actually do better in a top money market fund than in most growth stock mutual funds. What do you think about that?

That's absolutely true, but in a limited set of situations. When the stock market collapsed just a few years ago and inflation and interest rates were high, you could certainly make more through money market interest than through common stocks. So it's necessary always to remain flexible enough to take advantage of such circumstances. But those market conditions were unusual. In most cases, it's best not to rely solely on growth of your portfolio through interest-bearing investments.

Even in those hard, unusual times in the middle and late seventies, there was another investment that did quite well, real estate. Let's now move on and see how this staple of wealth and status might fit into your personal portfolio.

14

Before You Rush into Real Estate . . .

In 1949 a friend of mine purchased a large house in Connecticut—seven bedrooms and three baths—for $20,000. Down through the years he enjoyed considerable income tax deductions for local real estate taxes, mortgage interest, and the portion of the house that he used as an office. Thirty years later, he sold it for $154,000 and, being over age sixty-five, he was allowed the first $100,000 of his profits tax-free. The appreciation of the home perked along at an annual rate in excess of 7 percent compounded—not bad when you consider the low inflation and interest rates during much of the fifties and sixties. Then, when you add in the tax benefits, the yearly rate of appreciation goes even higher.

In the retirement clusters throughout the West and South, many other senior citizens can tell dramatic stories of how the old family homestead, more than just keeping pace with inflation, provided them with a hefty stake for their declining years. So, when you think of real estate as an investment, think first of your own home.

For years my wife and I lived in an apartment in San Francisco, and I long argued that renting was the only way to go. I wanted to divert as much capital as possible to high-growth areas of the market. My wife felt otherwise, and in the end she won. We bought a home. She not only won; she was right.

Just possibly, I might have made more money by buying in the stock market rather than in real estate. But it would not have amounted to much of a difference, and we would have sacrificed an investment in *living*.

After all, there comes a time in your life when you should not consider that everything you do must be geared to the maximum rate of return. As a complete person, and most especially if you have children, your first real estate investment should be a home of your own. Afterward, if you still want to pursue this form of investment, consider these two possibilities:

- Real estate investment limited partnerships
- Real estate investment trusts (REITs)

We'll consider each of these types of real estate investment in turn, with some practical suggestions about how you might employ them in your personal portfolio.

The Limited Partnership Ploy

Through stockbrokers you can buy a limited stake in a real estate investment partnership. These devices were created and packaged about ten years ago by nonbroker professionals specializing in real estate. Then they were merchandised to the general public, mostly through stock brokerage firms.

The firms became the general partners in the enterprise, and the individual investors were the limited partners. Under this arrangement the general partner bears full liability for the operation of the partnership, but also retains total control. The limited partners participate in profits and tax write-offs, and their liability is limited to the amount they have invested.

The limited partnerships became so lucrative that more and more brokerage firms offered their own packaged partnerships.

They came to represent a sizable part of some firms' income, and little wonder: Many of them are unconscionably loaded down with fees.

A while back I analyzed a number of these partnerships and found that up to 25 percent of the monies raised for the fund were dissipated on various kinds of fees. In other words, only 75 cents of every dollar actually went into real estate on behalf of the investors!

Many people rush into such investments because they are blinded by the tax deductions, especially in the first year. But if you are going to be hit by such outrageously high fees, you are better advised to give your money to charity, rather than to some promoter.

My first piece of advice is this: Carefully read the offering circular on a partnership to determine whether you are getting a fair shake.

When the brokerage firm sells as a general partner to its clients, we come back to the old story of conflict of interest. For the firm there are so many built-in incentives! It's once again a case of the investor taking all the risk while reaping little reward. And the higher that risk, the greater the reward to the brokerage firm and to the broker.

Once you determine, however, that your investment is not gobbled up by fees and commissions, these limited partnerships can be a good thing. The reason: Down through the centuries real estate has proved its worth in spades.

One thing I like about them is that you are not personally involved in the management. For example, you don't have to spend all your time finding tenants or replacing light bulbs. If you try to manage your real estate investments yourself—in apartments or other forms of leasing—you will find it a most time-consuming and exasperating experience. Nobody loves a landlord.

Help is on the way, I am happy to report, to solve the problem of the high fees and commissions extracted for limited partnerships. Within the next five years you can expect to see the advent of no-load real estate investment partnerships, efficiently merchandised by various discount brokers. The costs will be cut and the savings passed on to investors in the form of lower transaction costs. It is part of the same evolution that we have seen in the ongoing transition from load to no-load mutual funds.

The REIT Route

Another avenue of entry into real estate securities is through the REITs, or real estate investment trusts. A few years ago they were caught up in the high-interest crush, and many of them went through the wringer and dropped out of business. Today, though, REITs are on their way back.

In contrast to the partnership format, these investment vehicles are set up as trusts. This means that they take a sum of money and lend it to real estate ventures. Thus, they are a fixed-income investment and are usually not involved in holding equity interests.

There are mortgage-backed REITs that will give you a fixed rate of return. Those few REITs that involve equity interest do offer some opportunity for appreciation. Usually, though, you will not enjoy any of the tax deductions that the investment partnerships provide during the early years.

If these two broad areas of investment don't particularly appeal to you, there are other ways to get into real estate:

- You might find a number of listed securities that are in the real estate development business. But before you put your money in, study their background, management, and future prospects, just as you would analyze any stock investment.
- There are also ways to invest in mortgages that are held by banks or various other businesses operating in real estate. Sometimes the interest rates on these holdings can be quite high, and there is often considerable security because the land lies behind your investment.

Whatever form of real estate you may pick, I would advise you not to get into a rush. If you get into too big a hurry, you may make a big mistake. In particular, you should determine whether the investment you are considering is subject to one or both of two drawbacks that often accompany the outright purchase of a tract of land.

Drawback 1: Real estate typically lacks liquidity. If you need your money quickly, you may find yourself in a squeeze trying to sell or mortgage certain types of real property. Inevitably, the person who is trying to sell his real estate fast, and under considerable pressure, loses money.

Limited partnerships may also lack liquidity. Before you get into one, be absolutely clear about how you can get out. In fact, the only kind of real estate investments that you may be able to buy and sell fairly quickly are shares in a REIT or a public corporation that deals in real estate.

Drawback 2: If you decide to sell real estate you bought long ago—such as your home—you will have to buy or rent your next piece of property with *today's* dollars, not the more valuable dollars that bought you your old place. It may seem to you that you are getting a great profit, and perhaps you are, but if you want to put your payoff into other real estate, don't expect anything much better than the property you just sold. In fact, you may actually end up with less.

That was the painful experience of my Connecticut friend who sold his home for $154,000. Later, when he wanted to buy a small condominium, he looked high and low, but the best he could find was an apartment with only two rooms, a small kitchenette, and a bathroom—for almost $60,000.

Real estate, then, may be an important part of a personal investment strategy. In fact, at some point, for most people, it usually becomes an essential part. But with its lack of liquidity and other limitations, real property should comprise only a part, certainly not all, of your portfolio.

15

The "Treasure Chest" Investments

GOLD . . . silver . . . diamonds . . . coins . . . art . . . antiques. Human beings have treasured them, hidden them, stolen them, and fought over them down through the centuries. Kings have been ransomed with them; countries have been bought and sold with them. They have also been the centerpiece of great works of literature: How could Robert Louis Stevenson have written *Treasure Island* without the mystique of pieces of eight? What would the Count of Monte Cristo have been without the chest of jewels and precious metals that catapulted him from poverty to power and prominence?

Despite their historical glamour, how important a position should these valuables occupy in your investment portfolio? Should you turn your safe deposit box into a treasure chest?

Before we answer these questions, let's get a perspective on these "treasure chest" investments. Like real estate, they are what I call tangible investments, as opposed to intangibles like the pretty pieces of paper we call stocks, bonds, and securities. In times of inflation the tangibles do rise appreciably, even wildly. Gold may be especially volatile. Or consider the astronomical prices fetched periodically at Sotheby's by the old masters and modern art. Have we suddenly become a nation of passionate aesthetes? Of course not. Like the precious metals, these art works ride a crest created by fear of inflation. And what goes up with fright or inflation can come abruptly down again with a whiff of economic security or stable prices.

To put it bluntly, I don't see any of these "treasure chest" investments as long-term investments worthy of your portfolio. Here are some reasons I suggest that, in general, you stay away from them:

- the high cost of insurance and storage
- the necessity for expensive security
- the loss of interest or dividends on such frozen assets
- the uncomfortably high possibility that you will be cheated out of your money by counterfeiters, forgers, or larcenous metals dealers—if you're not first looted by burglars

I don't want to write off these investments without a more complete explanation, because many people get involved in them. In some unusual cases, they may even warrant a small place in your portfolio. So let's consider the major ones a little further.

Gold rose dizzingly in the early seventies, and the "gold bugs"— those fanatics who almost worship the yellow metal—thought all their adoration had proved justified.

But that was merely an historical aberration, because gold had previously been kept at a too low price by the arbitrary regulations of the federal government. That's no longer true. Gold now rises and falls—mostly falls—with the ebb and flow of the free market system. Antiques, coins, diamonds, and silver behave much the same way.

There have also been several major scandals and swindles associated with gold bullion. The most lurid involved a Los Angeles dealer whose firm had about thirty-five thousand trusting customers. They purchased the metal, which was supposedly snugly stored in a granite mountainside outside Salt Lake City.

Problems developed, however. The New York State Attorney General began poking into the situation, and about the time that this prosecutor went to ask the dealer for information on his accounts, the dealer was found dead in his sauna. A hose linked to a motorcycle engine was the apparent cause of death.

Subsequent investigations into the dealer's bankrupt firm indicated that he had funneled $56 million of his customers' gold into his own bank account. Not only that, but before making several trips to Switzerland, he had withdrawn millions; and he had also lost $10 million on commodities speculation.

Unfortunately, most gold coin operations of this type are largely unregulated. They are exempt under federal and state law because the deals are in precious metals. So you must beware! Many scams flourish in these unpoliced areas.

So, whenever anyone solicits you by phone on a "hot line" and offers a "special deal" in gold, be more than cautious. Most of these castles in Spain wind up as a cabin in the sticks for the investor. And don't expect the government to protect you; protect yourself against your own gullibility and greed.

Assume, though, that you've investigated a potential gold investment, and everything looks on the up-and-up. Unfortunately, even then you can get ruined. I can recall when gold hovered in the $100 to $150 range and later shot up to $850. At this writing gold is at about $400 an ounce, only half its peak value. I'd hate to think that I had risked a significant portion of my assets on gold when it was selling near the top, because now my estate would be worth less than half what it was just a few years ago.

Many people invest in gold out of fear that a major financial crash will cause most other investments to become worthless. With this scenario in mind, some advise having enough gold in your basement to get you through several months of hard times when the crash comes. If you're smart, the argument goes, you'll have extra gold on hand to buy things with your precious metal that other people can't.

Somehow, though, I can't quite see a person going around with a treasure sack, trying to buy bread by chipping slivers off a gold bar. That seems a little preposterous, just a little off the deep end, don't you think?

Silver also underwent a meteoric rise a few years ago, followed by a precipitous drop. The cause was the wheeling and dealing in the silver market by the wealthy Hunt family of Texas. The Hunts attempted—and succeeded for a short time—to corner the world market in silver. The price soared to the skies, in the $50-per-ounce range.

As of now, of course, the price has gone right back down again and is fluctuating between $8 and $10 an ounce. So, in a matter of just a few short years, silver is down about 80 percent of its peak. How would you like to lose 80 percent of your personal holdings?

The Hunts' run-up was just a bubble in an otherwise more stable market. But when the bubble burst, a lot of people got hurt. In fact, the debacle destroyed at least one brokerage firm.

Diamonds may be full of glitter and romance, but I would buy them only as an investment in "life," as jewelry that expresses special feelings between you and your loved one.

Jewels as a storehouse of investment value? Not on your life. Don't tell your wife or lady friend, but diamonds definitely are *not* a girl's best friend. They are among the worst places that a woman or man can invest her or his hard-earned capital.

First of all, they have little or no liquidity. Also they provide no income. But they *do* require heavy security, insurance, and other headaches. If you doubt this, look back at newspapers of the past couple of years in some of our nation's large cosmopolitan centers. There are more jewel thefts in hotels and private residences than will make you comfortable.

Furthermore, there tend to be high spreads between the bid and asked prices for diamonds. As a result, you will be lucky if you can ever recover your purchase price if you should lose one of these lovelies.

Recently, we've seen diamonds career through an erratic

market cycle. Just a few years ago they reached an apex of unwarranted popularity. Almost everyone wanted to own diamonds, and many hucksters got into the business of selling them. In the end investors lost millions of dollars when values plummeted 50 percent, 60 percent, and even 70 percent.

These gems are, in effect, controlled by the DeBeers company in South Africa, who largely regulate their supply. The DeBeers people would like to have prices appreciate nicely, not extravagantly every year. But the recent run-up got out of their control, and a market frenzy took over.

People actually thought that one-carat colorless, flawless diamonds were going to be their ultimate investment storehouse. As a result, prices got up somewhere in the price range of $60,000 to $70,000 per carat. Now, however, you can buy for about $18,000 per carat.

That's about all I want to say about the "treasure chest" investments, except to remind you that they are *not* the sort of thing you should treasure. But before we go on, there's another related form of investment we should consider, commodities.

Commodities, or futures, as they are also called, are contracts traded on an exchange that state a future date of delivery or receipt of a certain amount of a particular product. The products may be agricultural products, such as wheat or pork bellies. Or they may be metals or financial instruments. Speculators generally invest in these contracts at a price that they hope they can turn into a profit when the actual commodities are delivered.

My advice: *Please avoid commodities as you would a highly contagious disease!* The only exception I can think of would be if you were a cattle farmer, grain grower, or other expert in a commodities field and you understand precisely how the ups and downs of this savage market were likely to occur.

A particularly insidious feature of this market is that in commodities trading you can lose *more* than your investment. That was the big problem presented in the popular movie *Trading Places,* with Eddie Murphy and Dan Aykroyd. It could well become your problem, too, though in your case there won't be any playacting.

When you buy commodities, you usually do so on margin, by putting up only a fraction of the value of the contract. Let's say you are dealing in a contract worth $100,000. The margin might be only $5,000: You would be able to put up $5,000 to control a contract amounting to $100,000.

This game is always played with high margin, which affords huge leverage. For real swingers in the market, this style of investing can provide some of the greatest thrills because you're on a high wire, far above the gasping crowd, with not even a wisp of a net underneath.

Now let's go one step farther with our illustration. The value of the contract moves down in value from $100,000 to $95,000, but there have been no trades. The price merely dropped the allowable limit for a single day.

Finally, the first trade possibility comes in, at $90,000, and you grab it because you want to be rid of the infernal thing before it goes down farther, say, to $80,000. You have not only lost your $5,000 investment, but also an additional $5,000. Furthermore, you have to come up with the difference or be sued for it.

Finally, as I'm sure you're already surmised, this is a nickel-and-dime example I've presented, mainly because I didn't want to scare you to death. Suppose you delayed getting out of the investment and your commodities contract plunged right past $80,000 and toward the lower depths. You could be wiped out financially before you really know what's happening.

So, again I say that unless you are a farmer, rancher, or specialist in commodities, stay away! Go to Las Vegas instead of trying to win at this dangerous game.

Before I wind up this discussion, I'm going to relent a little on my hard line against the "treasure chest" philosophy. Let's return to gold for a moment. That metal has been the strongest lure for humankind as the ultimate in financial protection, the premier symbol of wealth. It's a sort of metallic Rock of Gibraltar for many people and serves to allay their deepest fears when they have just a little of it.

All of us need the kind of stroking gold can sometimes provide. So if you just don't feel right about not having a piece of Fort Knox, I would like to suggest a reassuring alternative to tying up your funds in the metal itself. Take not more than 5 percent of your assets and buy shares in some gold manufacturer or mining operator, such as Homestake in the United States, Dome in Canada, or one of the South African companies.

There are also no-load mutual funds that specialize in investing in securities of precious-metal manufacturers and mining companies. With one of these you will at least enjoy some current income. And if by chance gold really does run up again in value, you will participate in the windfall.

Right now, except for the truly believing "gold bugs," the kingly metal is out of phase, and out of the news. So if you're dead set on making an investment in gold, it is certainly much better to do so now than to wait for another frenzied period of the sort we experienced a few years back.

16

Investing Overseas

In Australia there are the media stocks. Sweden has high-growth drug companies. Japan offers the electronic companies.

For many stock traders these days, the action is overseas, where a new type of international mutual fund is creating many opportunities for high returns on foreign stock markets. To participate, all an investor needs is $400—and a willingness to accept a certain amount of risk.

Last year, and so far this year [mid-February of 1984], these international mutual funds have outpaced domestic equity funds. . . .

When compared with the standard barometers of market performance, the international funds show a significant return on investment.

THE ABOVE are words of wisdom from *The New York Times* written in early 1984—and I heartily concur today. American investment in companies that are domiciled outside the United States will continue to grow. We're just in the early stages of understanding this market, but we're getting more international all the time in our thinking and more interdependent with the rest of the world in every aspect of business and trading.

There's a growing understanding of the value of diversification of your investments outside the United States, and for a practical reason: We are finding some parts of the world experiencing much higher rates of growth—real growth—than the United States. For example, Japan, Singapore, Thailand, and Korea are all enjoying very high growth rates. In contrast, some areas of Europe are not having as much luck.

In some parts of the world the growth rate has been averaging well in excess of *double* the U.S. rate in the past ten years. Furthermore, some experts are predicting that this growth will continue at a much higher rate in the years ahead.

So how can you get a piece of this action?

Two avenues of foreign investment are open to you: the securities of other countries and their currencies.

In stocks, the highest quality of foreign securities—such as Royal Dutch, Sony, and Hitachi—are traded on the New York Stock Exchange. So you can buy individual shares right here. Or you can do foreign business the old-fashioned way, through buying American Depository Receipts (ADRs) for a number of the larger European or Japanese securities. The ADRs are domiciled in the United States, may be purchased through ordinary brokerage firms, and are subject to our taxes.

If you know about a particular security or you have some special knowledge of a country, you may be well equipped to buy these stocks independently. But if you aren't an expert in your own right, you may want to try one of the mutual funds that specialize in overseas securities. This is probably the most convenient way to obtain diversification and professional management at low cost. At any rate, that is the way I would do it if I were you.

As of the end of 1983, nine international funds, with $559 million in investments, were registered with the Securities and Exchange Commission.* While this total is tiny compared to the $104.4 billion in the mutual fund market, it is up sharply from

*The mutual funds investing overseas include Templeton Foreign; Trustees Equity-International (Vanguard); G. T. Pacific; Transatlantic (Kleinworth, Genson); Scudder; Kemper International; T. Rowe Price International; Merrill Lynch Pacific; and Canadian (Calvin Bullock). Also Lipper Analytical Services Inc. rates them according to their performances in the market.

the $314 million of the previous year, perhaps an indication that the foreign funds are increasing in popularity. One authority in the field believes that $100 million of the total represents return on investment, with the remainder being the result of a "significant growth in sales."

Why is foreign investing becoming more popular? Here is one good reason in a nutshell, as expressed by Ann Margaret Ulrich, director of institutional marketing at Templeton Foreign: "There is growing recognition that nearly 50 percent of the world's equity market lies outside the United States—and therefore 50 percent of the opportunity is outside the United States."

According to A. Michael Lipper, president of the Lipper organization, overseas expansion is "either just beginning or hasn't begun yet," whereas the American economy "is ahead in a time phase—it expanded first, very rapidly, and later slowed down."

However, I don't want to convey the impression that it's all champagne and roses, with no future prospects of ceilings on high growth in foreign securities. You have to look at each country individually and evaluate each one differently.

One mark against many foreign companies is that they don't have to follow the same disclosure requirements for financial information that our federal statutes demand. So you will find less data in their financial literature on which to base a judgment. Although many foreign countries are becoming more uniform in their laws as they attempt to attract outside capital, they still have a long way to go in cleaning up their accounting and reporting standards.

Another negative factor stems from the fact that many of the foreign markets are small. As Mr. Lipper points out, a modest volume in trading can generate a significant price change. Just a few investors getting out of a foreign stock may quickly lower its value.

A third possible negative is the strength of the dollar. If it remains strong, some authorities say, U.S. companies that export to other countries could benefit. On the other hand, with any major weakness in the dollar, foreign currencies will rise in relation to it and the overseas funds will benefit.

Now, what about investing in foreign currencies?

Some investors have been moving in this direction, as they put their dollars into German deutsche marks, Japanese yen, Swiss francs, or other monies. But why the popularity of this type of investment? Back when there was a regulated financial industry in this country, there were some real advantages, but now that deregulation has arrived, interest rates in the United States will pretty much take care of any differential that may have favored speculation in another currency.

So I'm not too bullish on investing in foreign currencies. Of course, you can, if you wish, place your money in a money market fund that handles a basketful of currencies. But these currencies usually fluctuate with the inflation rate and the interest rate of each economy; in fact, you can usually get better action with an ordinary American money market fund or certificate of deposit. So I don't see much advantage in spending time and money on the foreign currency market.

But if you're very cautious about the outlook for our economy—in fact, if you're in a state of near terror and you feel our currency is about to collapse—here is a suggestion: You might open up some kind of Swiss account by finding the local office of a Swiss bank. Then you'll have some of your money out of the U.S. economy, and protected in case it collapses.

Of course, I'm speaking somewhat ironically. If this is really your attitude, you see what you're doing, don't you? You're simply doing a "security number" on yourself. You're sacrificing current high yield and growth potential to give yourself a hedge against an ultimate disaster, such as a currency collapse. That's a big sacrifice for such a remote possibility.

But if it makes you sleep better, put a little in Swiss francs. Just make sure it's only a little. The interest rates over there are extremely low, and if you tie up too much of your cash this way, you'll have no chance at all to build up a good personal asset base.

This subject is especially interesting to me because it suggests a reason why the dollar has consistently been so strong in the world markets. Sure, you have some people in this country who want to concentrate their investment activity on foreign currencies, but most savvy investors elsewhere in the world are more interested in the dollar and our own domestic investment markets. Why is this? One reason is simply that we're the bastion of free enterprise, and everyone knows it.

But there's another, more emotional reason, and this brings us back to one of our main themes, the psychological dimension of every investment and market. You see, we make it easy for people to take their money out of this country. So what happens? All the money tends to come to us. It's a kind of reverse psychology: You tell people they are free to leave you, and the first thing they want is to be around you.

That's what happened in Hong Kong. This little economy has had an incredible growth rate, even though they have no natural resources other than their people. Yet they have had a burgeoning economy like you wouldn't believe, all because they have no restrictions on their money flow. I suspect things will probably change when Hong Kong's lease expires in 1997 and it becomes part of mainland China. But, still, what has happened there could occur in most other economies that dared to try a similar approach.

My final thought on foreign currency investments is this: The bottom line is not to spend too much time worrying about currencies unless you own a bank, work in a foreign exchange, or sell electronic equipment to France. There's no mileage in it.

17

Gimme Shelter!

To anyone in the higher income tax brackets, giving yearly unto Caesar (a.k.a. Uncle Sam) the things that are Caesar's seems cruelly disproportionate. So, for many, reducing the income levy becomes almost a holy mission. Hence, the widespread popularity of tax shelters.

But there are those who would like to huff and puff and blow down your tax shelter because many of them are no more substantial than the proverbial house of straw or sticks. Recently on television, one such "big, bad wolf"—a high IRS official—came on strong about what his examiners would be red-flagging as they double-checked tax returns:

First, tax shelters.
Second, tax shelters.
Third, tax shelters.
And fourth, tax shelters.

I had the feeling that he was trying to send us a subtle message.

While I share the general distaste for the tax collector, I must concede that the IRS had a point when it jumped on tax shelters such as the following:

- An equipment leasing firm in Massachusetts that promised a $101,523 tax savings on a $50,000 investment for taxpayers in the 50 percent bracket.
- In New York, a deal in so-called topical stamps. They were somewhat like postage stamps, but not the real thing, and offered a $4 write-off for each $1 of investment.
- A resort condo near Austin, Texas, that claimed investors could take off $7 for every $1 investment in the first seven years. The first year there was to be "deductible" interest of $36,680, compared to the measly $3,150 a homeowner could get on his house mortgage.
- The recent case involving a group of celebrities who lost all their money on one shelter. Nor was that all. They also got called on their promissory notes and the letters of credit that they had put up.

Today, the IRS has developed much sharper teeth than ever before in its war against "abusive" shelter deals. A somewhat dismaying statistic for anyone contemplating this form of tax deduction recently caught my eye. No less than 325,000 cases naming promoters or investors or both were pending in IRS hearings or in the courts!

Instead of just catching these "abusive" deals through hit-or-miss examination of individual returns, the tax boys can now go after the promoter almost from the inception of the scheme. First, they procure a court order. Then, through examination of the promoter's client lists, they can proceed against his pigeons, excuse me, his investors.

A comparatively new weapon of seeking injunctions to nip such deals in the bud is helping the IRS "turn around" this form of deduction, reports IRS Commissioner Roscoe L. Egger. Moreover, under a 1982 law, the service can justify its petition for an injunction when a tax shelter's valuation statement exceeds 200 percent of the proper asset value.

Retribution may come swiftly or after months or possibly even years, with attendant penalties and hefty interest arrears. When you invest in a shelter, it seems there's always an ax hanging over your head.

Of course, I'm not suggesting for a moment that you should totally "write off" all write-offs from your investment and tax planning. But I am warning you to be exceedingly wary because changes in the law and in methods of enforcement have made shelters somewhat less attractive and more risky.

Probably the safest tax shelters these days are real estate investments and a few of the more conservative oil and gas ventures. But how, exactly, can you tell if a deal is conservative?

For one thing, it's conservative if it's not leveraged. You put up one dollar and that dollar goes entirely into the project. If it's oil or gas, your money goes right into drilling a hole. You're not paying a dollar and expecting five or ten dollars worth of benefits.

Second, you should try, above all, to go in with an operator who can show you a good track record in this specialty. If the investment is oil or gas, he should be able to demonstrate that he's really struck some wells, and he's continuing to strike them on a regular basis.

The more reliable operator will drill in existing fields, and if he hits something, the return may be rather nominal. Perhaps you'll receive back your original investment plus an annual return of 10 to 20 percent. At least you'll get that much *if* he hits. If he doesn't, your investment is wiped out.

The more speculative operators, in contrast, will drill in exploratory fields; that is, they wildcat. If they hit, you'll enjoy a considerably larger rate of return, including your money back. But the risks are commensurate with the possible rewards.

I've been there myself in oil and gas tax shelters, and I've shared the risk and often received nothing in return except my 100 percent write-off. I also have a number of friends who have been in them, and most have lost their investments.

Basically, it comes down to this: Few investors make much money in oil or gas today. As of now, real estate is considered the king of shelters, though the IRS is also looking more and more closely at this form of investment. In sum, I would recommend that you focus on real estate for your shelter activity.

So what steps should you take to protect your investment both from sharpshooters, who want your investment dollars, and the IRS, which wants to reduce your tax benefits?

First, make sure that you go in with good, honest operators who won't take all your money away in fees. They should have a concrete, successful track record, and they should not be the type who try to use a lot of leverage, or extra write-offs, for relatively small amounts of invested cash.

Some of the most imaginative deals, with large multiple write-offs, end up in disaster. Also, they draw extra surveillance from the IRS, with the strong possibility that various items of deductibility will be totally disallowed.

Second, in real estate shelters you should try to find reputable firms that package investment partnerships and wholesale them to the brokerage firms. The firm, in turn, sells them to their clients.

Let's say that at year's end you decide, "I need a tax shelter, or I'm going to have to pay $15,000 in taxes."

If you have a lump sum of $15,000, you can put it all into a real estate shelter and get approximately a $7,500 to $8,000 write-off if you're in the 50 percent tax bracket. This will immediately drop your taxable income considerably. In fact, it's likely your tax bill may drop from $15,000 to about $7,500. The result: You've saved yourself $7,500 in taxes.

Now, what will happen to your $15,000 investment? I only wish I could tell you. We do know for sure that probably 20 percent of it went to the shelter promoters. That knocks your actual holding down to $12,000.

If you get a rate of return over the next five years of 15 percent per annum, you will get your $12,000 back, plus a return of 15 percent. But in my sad experience I've found that the people who package and distribute tax shelters are the ones who make the most money. The buyers of tax shelters may save some taxes in the current year, but frequently they don't come out ahead, especially if they get into the more speculative variety of shelters.

So your major guiding principle, before you put any money at all into a real estate tax shelter, should be: *Make sure that you would go into it even if there were no tax benefits.* Look for what I call the "cash-on-cash return." That is, you should get both your original money back *and* a return on your money—in addition to the tax write-offs. Another important principle is to limit your shelter investments to real estate for the most part, with an occasional foray into oil or gas if you really have reason to think you're onto a potential winner. Even with real estate, which tends to be the best of the shelters, there are at least two disadvantages:

- The high cost of entry into the field.
- The lack of liquidity if you need to unload the investment quickly.

To minimize your risks with real estate or other shelters, it's a good idea to keep in mind the following "shelter dos and don'ts," which have stood me in good stead over the years:

Do sound out friends who can tell real success stories and point to actual performance on the shelters they are using. Follow their advice in contacting professionals in various related fields, such as lawyers, accountants, and brokers.

Don't, under any circumstances, listen seriously to any offer by some stock and bond salesman; stay far away from his rosy, high-commission advice.

Don't do business with an individual or group that is just entering the tax shelter business. There are too many land mines for those with experience. While the mistakes of the newcomer may be honest, you will be the one who pays for them.

Don't be seduced by the shelter syndrome just because it's the fashion in your income group, coffee klatch, or tennis club. This is a particular problem for those in the thirty-five- to fifty-five-year life-cycle stage. There tends to be an attitude that goes something like, "After all, *everyone* is into tax shelters. Why not me?"

Do limit your speculative tax shelter investments to the 5 to 10 percent of your portfolio that you devote to speculation. If you've also invested in a relatively conservative real estate shelter, you may then involve a higher percentage of your total holdings.

Finally, if you half expect to lose the money you put into a shelter, why not just give it to your favorite charity? You'll get the same complete write-off, and you'll certainly accomplish a great deal more good than lining the pockets of promoters.

18

The Independent Investor
and the IRA

IT's a game that almost anyone can play, a game that represents "the kindest thing the Government has done for wage earners since the repeal of Prohibition," as *Forbes* magazine (March 14, 1983) joyfully exclaimed. The source of all the joy and fun is the Individual Retirement Account, better known simply as the IRA.

This investment can be written off your income by an amount of up to $2,000 yearly (more when working or nonworking spouses are included). Once you've put the money into an IRA account, the interest and other gains on the investment are sheltered as the IRA grows. You can protect this money from taxation in your high-income years, and you pay tax only as you draw money out of your IRA after retirement, when you presumably are in a lower tax bracket and subject to much lower tax rates.

Let's assume that, based on the 1982 tax tables for joint returns, your marginal tax rate is 25 percent on an annual income of $24,200. If you put aside the top annual contribution of $2,000, your tax saving will be a cool $500. Of course, you could save up to $1,000 on your taxes if you're in the top bracket of 50 percent.

Here is how the money grows, assuming that the $2,000 maximum is deposited on January 1 of *each* year, at a compounded rate of 10 percent per year:

After ten years there would be a total of $35,062 in your account. After fifteen years you'd have $69,899. After twenty-five years your total would be $216,364. And, finally, after thirty years you'd have a grand total of $361,887. From these figures, you can see the importance of getting started *right now* with this investment because the greatest gains, through the power of the compounding effect, come in the later years.

Basically, there are three kinds of IRAs: (1) the *individual* account, in which you can deposit 100 percent of your compensation, if you desire, up to the $2,000 ceiling; (2) the *spousal* account, which puts a $2,250 ceiling for the working husband or wife, plus the nonworking spouse; and (3) the *rollover,* in which taxable payments from other qualified retirement plans or IRAs are placed in a special IRA.

Only very recently Congress has broadened the IRA so that *every* working person in the country can qualify. In the past employees of companies with pension plans were ineligible. Because of the new legislation, an additional 80 million individuals now qualify.

Yet a survey conducted by Cadwell Davis Partners, an advertising agency, has yielded these dismal results: Only 9 percent of 2,000 men and women who were interviewed had actually opened IRA accounts for their 1982 tax returns! Another 11 percent planned to do so, but you know how reliable plans are when it comes to saving money. Some 23 percent claimed they could not afford an IRA; and 35 percent maintained they weren't sufficiently well informed on the subject. This is unfortunate since the plan is elegant in its simplicity; it's a true, uncharacteristic marvel of easy-to-understand government action.

There's only one way to look at this important development on the American investment scene. In my humble opinion, those who pass up this opportunity are guilty of almost indictable stupidity! To pull together the maximum $2,000 figure, you need save only $38.46 weekly, or $76.92 biweekly, or $166.67 monthly. If that seems a little heavy, given your income and family responsibilities, how about halving the amount? In other words, save only $1,000 this year. That at least would give you something to put into an IRA, and the tax savings and compounding effect over the years could add a sizable amount to your retirement income.

As I recommended in an earlier chapter, even a person in his or her mid-fifties would be well-advised to start an IRA. It's an ideal depository for conservative, high-yielding securities or certificates of deposit. Even a few years' accumulation in this shelter up to your retirement age will help you considerably.

Despite all these obvious advantages, some investors still hesitate. They resist getting into an investment like an IRA because of certain objections that are bothering them. Here are some of the most common I hear:

Objection 1: I'm afraid I won't be able to keep up yearly contributions to my IRA. *Answer:* You don't have to.

Objection 2: I'm worried I'll suffer penalties if I want to switch investment. *Answer:* You can transfer your account from one investment to another without any penalty if you keep the money in certain types of organizations, like a single mutual fund family or a self-directed account with a brokerage company.

Objection 3: My savings will in effect be frozen in the IRA account, and I'll incur heavy penalties for premature withdrawal. *Answer:* True. If you pull out before age 59½, you will be subjected to a 10 percent penalty, and you must also pay ordinary income taxes on whatever you withdraw. You can't even go into debt with these funds; and you cannot pledge them for loans.

But none of this is nearly so serious as it sounds. Thanks to tax-free compounding, you will have a cash cushion in the account if you've maintained it for some years. That will help you cover any penalty or the tax that is due if you decide to withdraw prematurely. (*Note:* You *must* start withdrawing the year you reach age 70½.)

There are also significant benefits to having this money so protected. First of all, you'll be less likely to touch it for frivolous reasons. Secondly, by and large your creditors can't get at an IRA, though the money may be claimed in divorce or support proceedings.

So if you decide to put your money into an IRA, how should you go about it?

The most fruitful way is to deposit the full $2,000 right at the beginning of each year. If you can maintain that schedule for twenty years, your growth, at a rate of 10 percent annual interest compounded, would be $126,005. By contrast, if you make your contribution at the *end* of each year, your total will be only $114,550 at the end of twenty years.

In addition to this lump-sum method of investment, there are at least three other ways you can get money into the IRA. First of all, you may prefer to have automatic deductions taken from your paycheck, just as you may have done if you bought Government E Bonds this way in the past. Secondly, banks can automatically transfer funds from your checking account. Finally, there is the *self-directed* IRA account, which allows you to deposit whatever you please, whenever you please.

But now the question arises, *where* should I place my IRA? There seem to be three major candidates:

Candidate One: Insurance. Insurance agents will try to sell you annuities, and you know what I think of them. Thumbs down! In an insurance annuity that guarantees you lifetime income on your retirement, there are always some zingers to watch out for. Generally, competitive returns are guaranteed *just for one year*. Thereafter, a lower minimum rate is stipulated for the life of the contract. Also, like most insurance contracts, you may need a Philadelphia lawyer to understand it—since one of his buddies probably wrote it.

Candidate Two: Banks. The banks offer two- or three-year certificates for IRAs, and I have only slightly more enthusiasm for them than I do for insurance. True, they will guarantee you 9½ or 10 percent interest as of this writing, and that may be wonderful for two or three years; but at the end of three years you come into a period when interest rates may be up or down. If interest rates have gone up, that probably means inflation has taken hold once again. So your fixed-income investment, which is caught there like a sitting duck at 10 percent, is gaining little or nothing in real, inflation-adjusted dollars.

I prefer something with more flexibility, since your IRA is likely to be locked up for the long haul. So I turn to:

Candidate Three: Equities. For younger people especially, I feel it's far preferable to be in equities, such as common stocks or growth mutual funds. That's where the action will be if you believe that the American economy will expand.

Banks will make much of the fact that your retirement funds are protected up to $100,000 by the Federal Deposit Insurance Corporation. They assert that no nonbank IRA can offer such insurance, but look again: If you invest through a brokerage house, you are protected by the Securities Investors Protection Corporation, in case of liquidation of the brokerage firm, for up to $100,000 in cash and $500,000 of securities you hold.

Finally, when you are shopping about, trying to decide where to put your money, by all means ascertain the annual costs of maintenance, the setup fee, and the custodial fee. Generally speaking, banks don't charge fees. Also, discount brokers may not charge a setup fee, maintenance fee, or termination fee. But full-commission brokers are different. A survey of half a dozen of the largest brokerage houses disclosed that opening charges ranged from zero to $30; annual charges from zero to $50; and closeout fees from zero to $50.

But don't let all these details bog you down and prevent you from doing the most important thing: setting up an IRA fund somewhere. Don't lose the forest for the trees. As *Forbes* magazine said, the IRA is the kindest thing the government has done for us since Prohibition. By all means, take advantage of it!

19

How to Solve
the Margin Mystery

ONE of the most fascinating, least understood, most constructive and also most *destructive* forms of investment involves the use of debt. Maybe you prefer the nicer word *credit,* but that begs the issue. Whenever you buy something on credit, you are in debt. Never forget that! And depending on how you control this dangerous beast, you will prosper or go flat broke.

There is a whole menu of different kinds of debt, including consumer debt typified by what you owe the department store and various credit card companies. Installment-purchase debt, incidentally, carries the greatest cost in the form of the highest interest rates.

Of course, if you have no money and desperately need certain essentials (not frills or luxuries), there is no alternative. You've got to rely on what amounts to glorified usury or starve. But try, at all costs, to get yourself out of that no-win position as quickly as possible. Also, don't make new financial commitments until you have straightened out your budget.

Many of us use credit cards, and there are many opportunities to abuse them, but I wonder if you ever realized what an excellent form of debt they represent. You can actually go into debt without paying interest on the loan! This is possible because you enjoy a free float for one to thirty days. If you pay everything off at the end of the month, there is no interest charge. On the other hand, if you don't pay up, there is hefty interest at the rate of 19 or 20 percent per annum.

There's also another reason to use credit cards and otherwise make use of debt: It is important to establish a credit rating for yourself. If you're in your early twenties, have you tried to buy something on credit? The first time, it can be an extremely embarrassing and frustrating experience. Never having chalked up a track record for borrowing and repaying, you were probably turned down. Typically, when you most needed credit, you couldn't get it, no matter what your financial health.

So, early on in your career, if you haven't done so already, it's important to buy something, *anything,* on credit. You may not need to do this, but it helps you set up a record. Then repay promptly so your credit record will not be tarnished. Later on you'll have to rely on that record when you seek a loan for a house or car or you want to make some other major purchase.

But even as I tell you to get into debt, I also strongly advocate that you do it judiciously. It's tempting to overdo it. With a credit card you can enjoy things now that otherwise would have to be put off indefinitely if you relied on cash. Also, the fact that all interest on loans is tax-deductible may make credit seem more attractive than it really is. In other words, if you're paying $1,000 out in interest each year and if you're in the 50 percent tax bracket, you may rightly point out that you're really only losing $500 a year after you take your tax deductions for interest. But be careful that you don't allow the tax benefits to blind you to the fact you're still losing that $500!

Inevitably, though, you're going to be using credit at different points in your life cycle, so it's important to learn to use it wisely. Now I'd like to spend a few pages talking about one of the cheapest forms of credit available to the individual, the use of margin.

The margin option is a possibility in most substantial brokerage firms, including discount houses. Yet it's amazing to me that so few people use it or are even aware of it. At our firm, for example, only 5 to 10 percent of our customers have a margin account. I suppose that in years past, "buying on margin" got a bad name when a lot of people were wiped out in bear markets.

But traditionally, we brokers have not just been in business to buy and sell through straight cash transactions. There is also a lending function in most firms: to this end, large departments may be devoted to margin and compliance operations. Through these means, customers can bring in their securities and then borrow against them to buy more securities. Or they can withdraw cash against the securities' value for other purposes, such as car loans or for a child's education. Many people, even those who use brokerage firms, are not aware that they can borrow money for whatever use they desire.

Here is how it works. Assume you have $10,000 worth of securities, and you borrow $5,000 on your regular margin account. Every month we will debit your account for the amount of interest based on a monthly calculation. There is never a call date, never a term date for the loan as long as the required margin is maintained. You can keep it on the books as long as you like. Thus, as a consumer you enjoy the utmost flexibility as to when you want to pay off the debt. Of course, we brokers benefit because we're charging you interest.

Let's say that on this loan the interest payment is charged at a rate of 12 percent per annum. At the end of the year, if you still don't pay any interest back, you would owe $5,600.

Of course, the interest rate on a margin account does change from day to day as interest rates change; in other words, it's a variable rate. It could perhaps fall to 5 or 6 percent, or go up to 15 or 20 percent. But even at these higher levels, it would remain lower than the prevailing rates on other types of consumer loans, which would also be rising in such a market.

In addition to a competitive rate of interest, a loan on margin may be repaid at a time that is convenient to you—and that time may be never. You may want to stay in a perpetual debit or loan position, at least until some other form of borrowing becomes less expensive.

In turn, the brokerage firm is very happy with your relationship *as long as you maintain an adequate margin between the amount you owe and the value of securities the firm holds for you.* The minimum for the New York Stock Exchange is 25 percent, and various firms vary up from that amount, though they never dip below it. At our company, we have currently set 30 percent as the minimum margin we will allow on a regular margin account.

Now, suppose your account is at our firm, and your collateral stocks drop in value from $10,000 down to a point where they would represent only a 30 percent margin. For example, at the end of the year they might be worth only $8,000, and you might have accrued $600 in additional interest during the same period. In other words, your original $5,000 loan from your broker now stands at $5,600. Moreover, with securities worth only $8,000, your margin—or the difference of $2,400—is only 30 percent of the value of your underlying stocks, which secure the loan.

Now, you can expect a call from your broker. He will insist that you bring your free equity back to 35 percent to maintain an adequate margin. To achieve this, you can deposit additional cash or securities in your brokerage account, or you can pay off some of the loan.

One point you should be aware of in this discussion: Not all securities are "marginable." While there is no published exchange list of securities that qualify, those that tend to be ineligible are the ones that sell for less than $5 a share. Also, shares issued by a brand-new company that has not yet established itself may be ineligible; so may be those of an older corporation that is in some kind of financial trouble.

It may puzzle you why borrowing on margin should be a relatively cheap kind of debt to hold. But if you think about it, there are good reasons. First of all, a margin loan is a *secured* loan, in that there is personal property, in the form of securities, that backs it up. This greatly reduces the risk to the lender, your friendly broker.

When you buy a car or furniture or get a vacation or education loan, these are typically unsecured. Even auto and furniture loans pose problems to the lender if there is a default. The items must be repossessed, an action involving legal fees, and then they have to be resold. Meanwhile, the underlying property is depreciating in value, and the lender probably won't get his full value back.

On the other hand, stocks and bonds are highly liquid, so brokers, as lenders, are well secured. This assures a lower-risk loan, and so consumers are entitled to enjoy a substantially lower interest rate.

These, then, are some of the basics of the intelligent use of credit, and an overview of how the use of margin can fit into the scheme of things.

Now, let's suppose you get serious about starting to make use of margin in your own investing. You walk into a broker's office and if you've thought things through, you'll probably begin to fire at him a series of questions that may go something like this:

Q: How long does it take to obtain a loan on margin? Can I get one today? Do I have to fill out a lot of papers?

A: If you have already established a margin account, the procedure is practically instantaneous. You can just walk in and pick up a check at the brokerage office the same day. Some people also get a margin privilege when they open asset management accounts. In these accounts, for a certain minimum deposit, they are able to write checks on interest-bearing accounts that pay money market rates. They are also allowed to write checks on the value of securities they have deposited with the firm.

Q: It's like an overdraft?

A: Yes. Customers can even use a major credit card in some cases. They create credit when they want it.

Q: Is there a limit on how much of a loan I can write?

A: It depends on what your credit line is. The key is the level of your margin availability.

Q: Shouldn't I be conservative about the way I use this sort of credit?

A: I lean toward an aggressive use of credit—that is, credit for investing. I really believe in that, credit for investing in homes and in securities. But it's important not to go crazy with it. I almost went too far once, and I'm lucky I'm not paying off the bank to this day.

Q: I don't want to get too personal, but could you explain that?

A: Sure. My life is, literally now, pretty much an open book. This incident occurred back in 1961, when I was fresh out of business school and fancied myself a real market hotshot.

At that time everybody was talking about his or her success with stocks, and I loaded up like crazy. Then I leveraged as much as I could by borrowing from the banks. I thought I was riding the gravy train.

Then came the crash of '62. I got crushed. Just crushed. I could have lost everything; I could have been in debt to the banks to this very day. But I was lucky. Not smart, just lucky. I managed to convince my banks to let me hold on to the few shares I had salvaged. And, lo and behold, the new bull market took off! Later in 1962 I had been completely bailed out.

That was a cruel kind of learning experience, one which I wouldn't wish on my worst competitor. And that's why, at the beginning of this chapter, I likened operating on debt unwisely to a dangerous beast. So be warned.

Q: Even with margin, you have to pay back someday what you owe, right?

A: Wrong. You may never pay it off. But the more deeply you go into debt, the more carefully you have to keep watch. The stock markets go up and down without warning, and when you are using margin or leverage, they sometimes seem to go down when you least expect or want it.

Q: I occasionally hear horror stories of doctors and other professional people who make as much as $200,000 or more yearly and then get all tangled up in debt because they are living on $250,000. Hasn't debt been a two-edged sword more often than not?

A: Many people with high incomes have this sort of problem. There's really only one thing I can advise: They should determine their *disposable* income—the amount available after taxes and the like—and then spend accordingly. But that's a tough thing to do in this day and age because almost everybody, it seems, is living somewhat above his or her means.

Q: You think the main problem is the desire to keep up with the Joneses?

A: No. There are also a lot of people who make bum investments. Then, in trying to recoup, they stumble into some crazy tax shelter which requires loan guarantees. Suddenly, they get called on a note they have unwisely signed. Their $200,000 income then gets overmatched by a $250,000 "outgo."

Q: But with such great earning power, can't they just go to a bank to bail them out?

A: The bank isn't willing to lend them money. Ever try to borrow from a banker? You know the old story: He will only lend when he establishes that you don't need it. He certainly won't lend unless he has a high degree of confidence that you will be able to pay it off in a relatively short period.

Q: Okay, I've decided to take out a loan on margin from your brokerage house, and I'm going to borrow 50 percent on my pledged securities. Suppose they begin to slip below that, so that my margin narrows. What happens?

A: Like every other broker, we have certain minimum maintenance requirements, and if you begin to push them, we'll let you know immediately. But we won't get excited about a 50 percent margin situation. Our maintenance level right now for a regular margin account is 30 percent. In other words, your margin equity has to be at least 30 percent of the market value of securities held in your account. That's the point where we start getting hot and bothered.

Q: What, exactly, happens if I slip beyond that 30 percent margin level?
A: You'll get a phone call or mailgram requesting an increase in your margin to 35 percent by depositing additional cash or securities.

Q: Sell all I own?
A: No. Just enough to bring you up to point where your equity will amount to 30 percent of your total securities. If we have to liquidate your holdings, we'll sell enough of your securities to bring your equity up to 50 percent of your holdings.

Q: How does that work?
A: Take the previous example we were discussing. You had your $8,000 in stock and a $5,600 loan, which left you at the 30 percent margin level, or not enough by our standards. So we sell $1,000 in stock and apply that to your debt. Then you have $7,000 worth of stock left, and your debt has been reduced from $5,600 down to $4,600. We just continue to sell until we reach the point where the debt will be 50 percent of your total securities, whatever that point is.

Q: Or I can make the adjustment through depositing cash or other marginable stock with the brokerage firm?
A: Yes.

Q: If I should pay back $3,000 on a $5,000 loan, would I then just be paying interest on the remaining $2,000, or would I continue to pay interest based on the higher amount until the entire loan is paid off?

A: You'd pay only on the $2,000 balance, or whatever you actually owe.

Q: Is there any difference between the way different brokerage firms handle these transactions?

A: There are a lot of similarities because margin lending requirements are strictly regulated by the Federal Reserve and SEC rules. But there are differences in the amount of interest you can be paid and the fees that will be required of you.

Q: In effect, you're performing a banking function.

A: Yes. But it's more flexible. For example, you may find it worthwhile to try to negotiate with your broker on the interest you are being charged. Smaller accounts are assessed pretty much according to the policy of the firm. But some firms charge lower rates on sizable accounts.

Q: So it's a good idea to shop around?

A: Definitely. And you should.

Q: When you talk about 50 percent or 35 percent minimums on margin, are those industry requirements?

A: No. The industry requirement, as promulgated by the venerable New York Stock Exchange, is 25 percent. They say that's the *absolute* bottom level to which an investor can descend before he must take steps to beef up his margin. That is, he has reached the point where he owns only 25 percent of his margin collateral clear and free, and he owes an amount equal to 75 percent of the collateral to the broker.

Q: Can you still trade in a pledged security, one on which you have borrowed?

A: Absolutely. Obviously, though, if you sell it, that changes your equity position and your margin percentage.

Q: Are mutual funds a qualifying investment for margin accounts?

A: The Federal Reserve and SEC have given approval to do just that. Only a few brokerage houses offer this service at this point, however.

Q: How does leverage work on a margin account?

A: Many people use margin in a speculative way, to increase their investment power far beyond what would be available to them if they didn't borrow.

Q: Could you give an example?

A: The investor buys $20,000 worth of stock with only $10,000 in cash. The other $10,000 has been purchased with funds borrowed on margin. If it's a $20 stock and it goes to $25, he has made a very nice profit on the leveraged portion of it. By leverage, I mean that he has used other people's money ("OPM," in market parlance), that is, the broker's money, to increase his profits.

Q: Wouldn't it be dangerous to borrow all the way up to your margin limit?

A: I would never encourage a client to go beyond the limit of 50 percent. That's one of the reasons I keep coming back to that figure in this discussion, even though our absolute limit at Schwab is 35 percent and the NYSE's absolute limit is 25 percent.

It's impossible to predict the ups and downs of the market. You can generally tell whether it's a bull or bear market, but you can't anticipate many intermediate moves in a cycle. So it's important to be prepared for emergency contingencies with a cushion, whether in your brokerage account or in your bank account or safe deposit box.

Q: Is there any other rule of thumb you recommend that I follow in operating on margin?

A: Much of the risk with margin relates to the volatility of the securities in your account. Conservative, no-load mutual fund shares have very little movement from day to day. Neither do most utility-type securities. Certainly, you can use more leverage there, that is, you can move up toward my recommended maximum level of 50 percent. But with highly volatile securities, I would keep my borrowing down to around 25 percent of the total market value of my securities.

Q: Puts and calls and other options are certainly volatile. Is it a good idea to use them with margin buying?

A: You cannot buy puts, calls, or other options on margin. Even though an option does have some value, it can't be used to determine your total margin account. That's just part of the basic rules and regulations of the market.

Q: What's a typical way a person might really get hurt in buying on margin?

A: A very common way is that they may go into very volatile issues without much diversification. Then they leverage up. This is where investors tend to get hurt the most.

Q: Do you recommend different margin strategies for the various life cycles of investing that we have already discussed?

A: Yes, and here are some guidelines. In the first cycle (ages twenty-five to thirty-five) you can utilize some margin, perhaps with loans amounting to 20 to 25 percent of your equity account.

In other words, if you have $10,000 invested, you should have only a maximum of about $2,500 tied up in margin debt. That will give a little added firepower to your growth potential. But I would not go the full 50 percent unless you are *very* confident about the stocks involved.

Q: Any other caveats for the younger investor?

A: I wouldn't use margin until you have gone through at least one bull market and one bear market, and really know how you feel and act under fire. Some people can handle calamities and disasters in the stock market better than others. Others just panic and do strange things to themselves. I've seen people go completely haywire when it came their money.

Q: What do you mean?

A: Some people I know lost all control in down markets and sold out everything they owned. As a result, they missed the next bull market entirely. Some walked away permanently from the market after that, and they lost any opportunities to profit by their mistakes. Anyone with such a temperament who gets prematurely involved in margin trading will probably exercise very poor judgment under pressure. In such a state of mind there is a tendency to make all the wrong decisions about the use of brokerage debt.

Q: In the later life-cycle stages, don't most people have enough maturity and experience not to panic?

A: Perhaps. But certainly, as you get older, say, up into the fifties, margin carries a greater risk for you. You will be less able to make back capital that you have lost in an ill-conceived move to leverage your holdings. You're getting closer to retirement now, and so it's important to be more conservative. Consequently, I'd advise most older people to steer clear of margin buying.

Q: How about the peak earning years, in the thirty-five- to fifty-five-year life-cycle stage?

A: At this stage margin can be a very useful tool. You should be at your highest income level, and so all the interest you pay on your loans is tax deductible. Also, by now you should have had a number of years of experience in the market. Your portfolio should consist of a solid base of stable securities, and you may find that you can greatly increase your wealth through a wise use of margin trading.

Properly used, a margin account can provide many investors with an extremely useful line of credit at a relatively low interest rate. Certainly there are dangers, as there are with any use of debt, but if you follow some of the guidelines and heed the warnings we've discussed, I expect you'll find you're much better off with a margin potential than without it.

20

Fire, Flood, Fraud, and Failure: How Safe Are Your Securities?

LET's be frank. Safety preys on the mind of practically every investor in the still of the night, as he or she tosses and turns in bed. Questions keep popping in and out of the mind: Have I done all I can to protect my hard-earned stake? Is there perhaps something I don't know about that might rob me of my holdings?

So, just how safe, in the physical sense, are your stocks, bonds, and irreplaceable financial records in case of fire, flood, or earthquake? How safe are they from the collapse of your brokerage firm? How safe are they from theft or fraud by a broker?

Some brokers are reluctant even to bring up these issues. After all, there's the risk you might get so scared you'll turn tail with your money and put it all in your local bank. But you have every right to know what threatens your financial security, and what is being done to protect your valuable assets.

First let's deal with the *physical side of safety*. The best place to start is the lowly but popular safe deposit box. Is it really worth the $10, $15, or $50 yearly that it costs you?

For many individuals, that long, narrow strongbox, tucked away deep in a bank vault, represents the ultimate in protection of one's assets from theft, mutilation, destruction, and even one's own mislaying of records.

I'm not quite that enthusiastic. I use a box only for a few items like life insurance policies, the house deed, and certificates of auto ownership. Actually, in this modern age the best and most convenient storage house for the custodial care and record-keeping of your securities is a brokerage house.

Here are some of the pluses of the brokerage approach:

- You receive monthly statements from the broker listing all your security assets.
- Most of the firms will also provide valuation.
- They will collect your dividends or interest and credit them to your account.
- They will either send your earnings to you or, if you prefer, allow them to accumulate.
- In most cases, they pay interest on the credit balances that you have established, pending investment of the funds. Or, if you so desire, they will sweep them into money market funds.
- You need not worry about those precious pieces of paper, the securities themselves, being stolen, mutilated, or destroyed. They are placed in the Depository Trust Company in New York, a subsidiary of the New York Stock Exchange. Or they are put into deep vaults in other cities.
- Practically all the firms maintain duplicate records in vaults that are far removed from their home offices. These include locations like salt mines in Utah, which are fully protected from natural disasters such as fire, flood, or earthquake. In our own case, records are shipped out of our offices for such safekeeping within two days. This tends to be the general practice in the industry.
- As a client, you have your own record—a monthly statement—which would be evidence of ownership if all else somehow failed.

These are all obvious physical advantages that a brokerage firm has over the traditional safe deposit box. There's another benefit, though, that's at least as important: *convenience*.

Say that you are selling or adding to one of your positions. Your records and certificates will already be with the broker, so there should be no delay. You can liquidate a security with a phone call. It's far simpler and quicker than (1) going to your bank, (2) removing the security from your box, or (3) delivering it in person (with the attendant risk of theft or loss) to the broker's office.

In reverse, if you purchase securities, the brokerage firm will mail them to you, but you still have to transport them to the safe deposit box. Either way, the procedure is cumbersome, bothersome, and a bit risky.

In the case of very large accounts, estates, or trusts, some individuals prefer to employ the trust departments of banks as custodians. This poses some advantages, but also one big disadvantage. A brokerage firm usually charges little or nothing for the service. In contrast, a bank trust department will exact a fee of from ⅜ of 1 percent, without management, up to 1 percent, including management.

So suppose you decide to leave your securities with a broker. A question that I often hear, and one I want to be perfectly frank in answering (though this will definitely eliminate me as a candidate among my peers for Most Popular Broker of the Year) is: "For good record-keeping, can you trust the small discount houses or the small full-commission brokerage houses, as opposed to the large ones?"

My answer: It is critically important to do business with a firm that has efficient record-keeping. If their records are not current—or at least not corrected in a hurry—and a dispute later arises or something happens to the firm, there is definitely some risk to your investment.

Now comes the zinger: Usually, small brokerage firms arrange to have their back-office (record-keeping and administration) activity handled by a major brokerage firm. On the one hand, this may give you a certain feeling of comfort, to know that one of the "big boys" has a hand in the matter. On the other hand, I would feel somewhat apprehensive because there is now a third party involved in your relationship. The small brokerage firm really doesn't have total control over your accounts and records. If something goes wrong, where does the buck stop?

So, many times, if there is a problem, you might eventually have to take your complaint to a third party, with whom you are not familiar. This record-keeping firm has no personal relationship with you, and you may sense they don't care about you quite as much as they do about their other regular customers. So I advise investors to stick with the major firms that do their own back-office work.

This same back-office problem emerges, by the way, with some of the banks that have recently been getting into the discount brokerage business. Many of them don't do their own back-office operations, and they are not in control of their records. Yes, they may be very fine banks on one level, but they become dependent on a third party in brokerage processing matters. If the bank has only been in the brokerage business for a year or so, I would advise great caution in using it unless it boasts a fully integrated subsidiary brokerage operation.

Turning to man-made disasters, such as brokerage failures, I want to lay it on the line with you. In some dozen years there have been dozens and dozens of these failures from one coast to the other, from New Hampshire (one) to my own state of California (seventeen). At least two dozen states have been hit by these problems. The year 1981 was particularly disastrous for difficulties in our industry. There were any number of reasons, ranging from bookkeeping problems and inadequate capital to mismanagement and even one apparent large-scale fraud. Let me thumbnail a few illustrations:

- Several hundred customers were affected when a Miami stock brokerage firm failed because of inadequate capital.
- A related Los Angeles firm, with twelve hundred clients, also collapsed. There were charges of stock manipulation in both firms.
- In St. Louis, another brokerage house with more than four thousand accounts closed its doors. A senior vice president who

had risen from a lowly clerkship was accused of having milked the firm for $16 million. Then he allegedly bought a Florida horse farm, various condominiums, and even a Las Vegas hotel.
• In New York and New Jersey two more firms went belly up.

But wait, all is not lost in any of these situations. In fact, the "white hats" are riding to the rescue in the form of the Securities Investor Protection Corporation (SIPC), in which all the brokerage firms in the country must be enrolled. This organization paid out more than $62 million to the depositors and clients of these distressed institutions.

All told, in 1981 the SIPC came up with $100 million to bail out the innocent victims of brokerage stupidity or fraud; another $38 million in 1982; and a resounding $40 million in just one case in Ohio in 1983. In this latter case, the SIPC sleuths discovered that $5,000 in stock had been valued at $279 million!

The SIPC has been able to pay out almost a half billion dollars since its inception in 1970. Most of this has resulted from the skillful liquidation of the failed firms. But a quarter of the restitution money has come from the SIPC's own funds. Theodore H. Focht, the SIPC's general counsel, was able to report not too long ago: "In the vast majority of cases, customers get back 100 percent. The program has fully protected all but a few claims."

Although I've mentioned the SIPC in earlier chapters and also in this one, I think it deserves a fuller treatment for every serious, independent investor. After all, it's helpful for anyone's peace of mind to get as many facts as possible about those institutions and systems that protect us from harm.

This quasi-government organization was originally set up by Congress specifically for the protection of brokerage clients. All brokerage firms must join it, or they are not allowed to perform brokerage operations in the United States. The system is very similar to that of banks, which must be members of the Federal Deposit Insurance Corporation (FDIC) in order to obtain a charter. But as far as both the SIPC and the FDIC are concerned, I have heard the same unfounded worry expressed. People complain that only a small percentage of total deposits are actually within the FDIC. As a result, there has long been speculation about whether the federal government would really intervene if that insurance body ran out of money.

Nonsense! Of course the government would intervene! And I feel the same is true for the SIPC, although in its history since 1970 it has never depleted its resources. In that very unlikely event, my strong feeling is that the SIPC, already backed up by $1 billion in callable government loans, would receive another $1 billion, $2 billion, or whatever amount would be needed to resolve the crisis.

Since the SIPC and the FDIC are government-sponsored, it would absolutely devastate investor confidence or bank depositor confidence if either organization were permitted to go under. Thus, the argument that the FDIC assets cover only a small percentage of total bank balances, and hence the organization is vulnerable, represents a total misconception about insurance. The FDIC is just like any other insurance program. No insurance is ever 100 percent covered; the amount of capital and cash on hand must be based on the probabilities of things happening.

At this point, everyone who feels reassured by my explanation is invited to skip to the next chapter. But for those of little faith and still unconvinced, I'll put the SIPC on the hot seat by putting some further questions to a hypothetical representative from that organization.

A CHANCE TO GRILL THE SECURITIES INVESTOR PROTECTION CORPORATION (SIPC)

Q: How does the SIPC actually operate?
A: In the event of a failure, we may ask a federal court to name

a trustee to liquidate the firm. In some instances involving smaller firms, the SIPC itself may carry out the liquidation. In both cases, protection of the firm's clients will be similar.

Q: What happens to my account in such a firm?

A: Accounts may be transferred to another SIPC member firm, with which you may then deal; or you may transfer the funds to a firm of your preference. If an account transfer to another firm is not feasible, the customer will receive all securities registered to him.

Q: What if there are questions as to the accuracy of the records, or some similar objection?

A: On a pro rata basis, all remaining cash and securities held by the firm will be distributed to claimants. SIPC funds will satisfy remaining claims to a maximum of $500,000 (although on claims for cash the limit is $100,000). Assets remaining after liquidation may be used to satisfy any further customer claims on a pro rata basis with other creditors.

Q: What types of property does the SIPC protect?

A: Cash and most types of securities like notes, stocks, bonds, and CDs. But not unregistered investment contracts or any interest in a commodity, commodity contract, or commodity option.

Q: May a customer have SIPC-protected accounts with more than one member firm?

A: Yes.

Q: How about coverage for more than one account with the same firm?

A: Extra accounts in the same firm only qualify for coverage if the person maintains the various accounts in different capacities, such as for himself and as trustee for another person.

Q: Where are claims submitted?
A: To the trustee, if he has been appointed; otherwise, to the SIPC.

Q: Will a customer get back all the securities in his account?
A: Usually. If that's not possible, the customer will receive cash in lieu of the securities.

Q: How is the amount of a claim determined?
A: The sum will be *net equity*, which represents the total value of cash and securities owed to the customer, minus total value of cash and securities owed by the customer to the firm.

Q: Must a customer pay what he owes the firm to the trustee?
A: Usually, in computing net equity, the indebtedness is subtracted. But if the customer owes more to the firm than he is owed, he must pay the difference to the trustee.

Q: Who operates the SIPC?
A: Subject to Senate confirmation, the president of the United States appoints five of its seven directors, two representing the general public and three the securities industry. The Treasury and the Federal Reserve Board name the other two. Some oversight and regulatory functions are exercised by the SEC.

Q: Where does the SIPC's money come from?
A: A good question. At first SIPC members were assessed on their gross revenues from the securities business. After the fund

reached $150 million, $25 yearly assessments per member firm were fixed. By last year the fund had dipped to $144 million, and the assessments were raised on the seventy-two hundred broker-dealer members.

Q: Is any emergency financing in place?

A: I've already mentioned that borrowing up to $1 billion from the U.S. Treasury through the SEC could be permitted, if necessary. If assessments on the industry would not repay the loan, the SEC could impose a transaction fee on equity securities at a rate not above 1/50 of 1 percent of the purchase price, or 20 cents per $1,000. This would not apply to transactions under $5,000.

Q: Who oversees the operational financial conditions of SIPC members?

A: The stock exchanges and the National Association of Securities Dealers Inc. (NASD) serve as examining authorities for their members. The SEC performs the same function for SIPC members that do not belong to an exchange or the NASD. The SIPC itself has no authority to examine or inspect its members. It's not a regulatory body.

So how about it? Still unconvinced about the safety of the securities industry?

I can add only one thing more, O ye of miniscule faith: Most brokerage firms carry *additional* insurance beyond the SIPC protection. In our own case, Aetna covers an additional $2 million of securities per account, and for the most cautious investors we can even arrange additional coverage up to $10 million in securities.

For my money and securities, I feel safer with a brokerage account than with any other repository, including a safe deposit box. These boxes are not insured and are as subject to bank theft as many other banking facilities. So there's really no reason not to get into the stock market. It's really safer to get into the market than it is to cross the street.

21

The Investor's Guide to
Legal Troubleshooting

WHAT happens when you have a dispute with a brokerage firm?
In a nutshell, most firms that have been in business any length
of time will go out of their way to resolve complaints. Those complaints may come at a variety of levels, and some can be solved
very quickly. Here are a few easy ones:

Complaint: "I didn't receive my check on time."
A good brokerage firm will be able to tell you very quickly that
the check was sent on a certain date. There's probably a mail
problem. If necessary, the firm can stop payment and issue another check.

Complaint: "Where are my stock certificates? I purchased them
on August 1, and it is now September 15. *Where are they?*"
Typically, it takes three to five weeks for securities to be transferred and mailed to clients. If it takes more than six or seven
weeks, there is definitely a problem with the brokerage house, and

a phone call is in order. Most firms will be able to get back to you with a satisfying explanation for the delay.

Sometimes, transfer agents make mistakes, so the brokerage house has to send the securities back to them. Your settlement day is five days after purchase, and when there is a long lag in delivery, people frequently grouse in terms similar to the following:

Complaint: "That broker must be taking advantage of me, to take so long to finish this transaction!"

Not at all. You see, the broker *must* pay for your purchase on the fifth business day after he executed the order, so that the seller will receive payment on that fifth day. At this point, all the monies have changed hands.

What happens next, and usually causes the delays, is a blizzard of paperwork:

- A certificate will be transferred from the stock exchange organization to a transfer agent, with proper instructions. These indicate that the shares should be transferred to your name.
- After this is done via a transfer agent, the shares are transmitted back to the broker-dealer.
- In turn, the broker checks them and mails them on to you.

All these steps take a period of three to four weeks. The broker is *not* taking advantage of you. It's just the tortoise-slow system. Some sweet day, I hope, the system will be streamlined and we will be able to get away from stock certificates altogether. Investors might end up getting an IBM card instead. Meanwhile, patience, please!

If all this seems cumbersome and inefficient, it is. But some investors compound the delay by requesting that their securities be sent to them. About half of our customers do so. There's a whole world of people who are so old-fashioned that they like the look, the feel, and the smell of a stock certificate. They like to take it down to a safe deposit box and fondle it periodically.

As I said in the previous chapter, there's some risk in this procedure, but it's sometimes very difficult to change the attitudes of people, especially those who are worried about some brokerage firm that went under years ago. Perhaps they had securities in that firm and didn't get them back (before the SIPC insurance was set up). So you really can't blame them.

On the other hand, the newer generation in investors seems very confident in the strength of the typical brokerage firm and its backing by government-sponsored insurance. They know they are really taking no risk at all by leaving their securities in the custodianship of their brokerage houses.

But genuine gripes still arise. So let me now outline the proper procedure to follow when you run into real problems with your broker.

Step 1: With your account number in front of you, call your brokerage firm and explain the problem to the customer service-person. Nine times out of ten the complaint can be resolved on the phone in minutes or even seconds.

Step 2: In complicated cases you are best off writing a letter to the firm. All brokerage houses must, under regulations, maintain complete files of complaints, both for review by regulatory agencies and by stock exchange monitoring groups.

Step 3: Be sure that you address your letter to the manager of the branch of the firm where you do business. If you send it to the headquarters, it will just have to be passed back to the branch, and you'll lose more time.

In most situations this is as far as you'll have to go. Usually, firms will try very hard to resolve the problem in favor of the client. I'll even go so far as to say that if the decision is 51-to-49 for the firm, the firm will still settle it to the satisfaction of the customer.

I don't pretend for a moment that this is pure altruism. It's mostly enlightened self-interest. No firm wants an irate or dissatisfied customer speaking badly about it. My own rule of thumb is: One angry customer can drive away five or ten potential new customers.

Thus you have real leverage against a firm that is worried about leaving a client dissatisfied. Of course, some people are chronic complainers, and you can do little or nothing to satisfy them. But with a legitimate complaint, any enterprising brokerage house will do handsprings to please the customer.

A corollary to the above rule of thumb, which I keep emphasizing to our own employees, is this: One out of every three of our customers comes to us by virtue of a referral. And we've never gotten a referral from an unhappy client. As with most discount houses, the nature and success of our business are basically dependent on the continual referral of customers. Sometimes, though, all the phoning, the letter-writing, and the moral and economic pressure on the firm to keep a customer happy just won't do the trick. So you have to hang a little tougher.

But let me free you of one mistaken notion. Some people think that in such a case it helps to report the matter to a regulatory agency, like the SEC. It doesn't. The reason is that the SEC is so busy with so many other things, they just don't have time for the small stuff. They may like to hear your complaint if it's serious enough, and then monitor it and warn the firm. But they have no power as such to make the firm pay you any money.

So what's the best procedure?

I would hire outside counsel and perhaps ask the firm for arbitration. Also, if your attorney doesn't specialize in this field, have him work with a lawyer with a history of handling securities issues to look at your problem. That way he'll be in a better position to make a judgment as to a possible claim.

Some problems that might justify the expense of retaining a high-priced legal specialist, if you can't solve them any other way, include the following:

- A firm employs high-pressure salespeople who are responsible for excessive turnover in your account. They "churn" it, as financial people would say, without your authorization.
- The broker exceeds his authority in buying or selling for your account.
- The broker buys an inappropriate security at much too great a risk, and it collapses.

- Let's say that you, the client, instructed the broker to sell out at the market price on one day. He thinks he can play it smart and get an extra half point. So he waits until the next day and is unable to unload at a decent price.
- I've seen many instances where the broker tried to play it cute, thinking he could mastermind the market on behalf of his clients. He honestly thought he was doing a good job for his clients. Actually, in many such cases the broker has no idea of what is happening in the market, and when he thinks the outlook is rosy, it's really collapsing under him.
- The client says, "Buy me some of those shares today." But the broker holds off, waiting to buy at an eighth or quarter of a point lower. Then boom! The market takes off, and he misses the whole move.

Fortunately, most discount brokerage firms—since they don't offer advice—are usually spared the problems of discretionary accounts. But we do have some cases where the clients honestly believed they put in a clear order to sell, when what they really said was something ambiguous like, "sell me some shares," an instruction that suggests they want to *buy* shares.

You can easily fall into disputes when the customer does not put in his order clearly and the broker-dealer does not repeat it back to him in clear English. Also, because most orders are by telephone, the disembodied human voice sometimes poses difficulties. In addition, there can simply be a problem with memory. So my advice to clients is: Make sure that you *really* listen to your broker. Also, ask him to repeat back the order to you. Then take detailed notes on what has been said. Just these simple precautions will keep you out of many legal hassles.

In the traditional full-commission houses many of the problems arise because their brokers are in such a hurry to sell securities that they don't bother to repeat back the order. If I were a client of any firm, I would *insist* on such a playback. Certainly, in our own firm this procedure has cut our mistakes by more than 50 percent.

In addition to insisting on repeating the order, there are four other keys I've discovered to prevent legal problems before they can happen. These methods focus on a close reading of the monthly statement.

In the first place, make it a policy to study the statement and be sure that all the figures look reasonable. You needn't waste time reconciling every penny, but double-check to see whether all your securities and dividends are listed. Although it's very rare for any investments to get lost, computers can sometimes do funny things. So it is only prudent to review your paperwork periodically.

Second, make sure that your order is placed in the correct account. Sometimes, if you maintain two or three accounts with one brokerage firm, such as an IRA, an individual account, and a joint account, problems can develop.

Third, be certain that the transactions you're credited with involve the exact stock you bought or sold. A common snafu is for a broker to put through a transaction listing a company with a name *similar* to the one you asked for, but not the same. Or, in the case of a company with several series of preferred issues or various kinds of related securities, he may become confused and list the wrong issue.

Fourth, as far as transactions involving transfers between different brokerage firms are concerned, be *very* careful.

We recently had an exasperating experience where we took a bum rap on a matter of this type. A customer asked us to transfer part of his account to another brokerage firm. Later we received a lengthy letter complaining that we had not transferred it fast enough, and that this delay had caused him any number of problems.

Well, we double-checked and found that we had transferred the account quite properly and promptly. The trouble was that the other firm had failed to credit the transfer to him. In this case, the mistake was finally caught, with no permanent damage. But the lesson for you is that it's absolutely essential to go through that monthly statement with a fine-toothed comb every time you get it.

Even as I recount all these mix-ups, however, I don't want to give you the impression that these are everyday occurrences in any brokerage firm. Because the brokerage business is a tightly regulated industry, all of the reputable firms will run regular internal audits to be sure their noses are kept clean. So the chances are that most problems can be resolved rather quickly, especially if you note any discrepancy rather quickly on your statement. In a really efficient firm, errors will appear on your statements less than 3/10 of 1 percent of the time.

Finally, many potential legal problems, especially those related to estates after a customer dies, can be averted if the investor just chooses the right kind of account while he's still alive. Here is a sampling of the types you can choose from:

The Individual Account: This one, as the name implies, is opened and owned by one person and is the most popular type of account in most firms. When you die, however, it will usually have to go through probate, and there will be delays in dispersing the moneys and securities. This account will be frozen even if someone tells us, "Hey! I'm the executor of the estate, and I have the papers to prove it. Now, how about taking my order?"

A broker can't take any order until the paperwork has passed through the firm's legal department and the department has given its okay. The legal eagles may well examine the necessary papers the very day they receive them, but then the matter has to go into probate. If stock is involved, most firms hold up the proceeds of sales until the transfer agents of the individual companies say, "All right, we have everything we need."

So there are some problems with the individual account upon the owner's death. But the next type of account can take care of this.

The Joint Tenancy Account with Rights of Survivorship: This is the simplest of all types of accounts to process at death, and it's the second most popular account that we offer. Generally, you'll have two owners named on this account. Then, if one of the parties dies, the securities and cash automatically go to the survivor.

For example, suppose a widow calls in and tells us, "My husband has died, but I would like to place a trade."

We could make that trade, though we do need a certified death certificate, and in some states we must file a consent to transfer. The account may thus be tied up briefly until this minimal paperwork is finished.

The Tenants in Common Account: In this type of account if one tenant dies, his portion does not automatically go to the other tenant. Instead, it becomes part of the estate of the person who has passed on. So the brokerage firm has to hold things up until they find out exactly how much of the account each tenant owned. It may have been a fifty-fifty arrangement, but there may also have been different percentage division according to the tenancy in common agreement.

The Custodian Account: Usually, minors would be the beneficiaries of this type of account. The way we set them up, there is one custodian and one child per account. When the minor reaches majority, the account can become his or her property.

We are quite careful to be sure that the Social Security number and date of birth on the forms match the actual ones of the minor. Also, we always check the age of majority in the state where the account is being opened. Sometimes, we find we have to say, "We can't open this as a custodian account because the minor is no longer a minor in your state."

Guardianship Accounts: Many clients become confused over the difference between custodian accounts and guardian accounts. Anyone can open a custodian account for any minor who is a relative. In a guardianship account, on the other hand, you must receive an appointment from a court and an authorization similar to letters testamentary in an estate account. All this involves a much more complicated procedure.

In addition to these accounts, there are a variety of others: corporate, sole proprietorship, irregular trust, family trust, IRA, investment club, and many more. We are finding increasingly that investors want estate accounts, too. If they are in the position where they must serve as an executor, they say, "Let the broker handle the estate."

So as you can see, there are many legal implications to being your own stockbroker. But if you stay reasonably alert in your market dealings from start to finish, you'll find the dangers to be more imagined than real. The great investment adviser John Templeton says that in the many decades he has been in the business, he has never sued or been sued. But he's a very careful man, and so, too, should you be.

22

How About a Little Spice
in Your Portfolio?

In the late 1960s I was enjoying considerable success in the stock market. Then along came an opportunity to invest in a venture called Computer Time Sharing Corp., a great new name in the swinging sixties, a really sexy stock, at least for a few fleeting moments.

I bought in at $5 a share, and within a year's time the company went public. My $5 stock was now worth the equivalent of $20 a share, and it rose shortly afterward to the equivalent of about $35 or $40.

I say "equivalent" because I was bound by a rule that required me to hold my securities for two years before selling. By the time I could sell, the stock had dropped to the "equivalent" of $1. It had a great short-term flight, but then it went into bankruptcy. Now, I use the pretty pieces of paper as wallpaper, to remind myself of the ephemeral nature of some exotic stock market successes.

I've seen, and taken a ride on, many such comets. They're fun and exciting for a while. It's the kind of thrill we all hope for in life, but I've learned the expensive way Rule Number One for spicy, speculative ventures: Limit your exposure if you decide to invest. Speculative stocks are almost always too hard to analyze properly. No "spice" in the market should be the core of your investing program.

I've flirted with some fantastic opportunities over a fairly long period of time, and I'd blush to tell you how many disasters I've put money into. They seemingly involved great ideas, smart people, and perfect timing, but, for one reason or another, they just didn't pan out. I've got a whole barnyard of these donkeys!

Once I invested in a scheme to put on the greatest animal show ever. It was perfect! The idea was to reproduce an outdoor scene that would suggest going through the jungle in Africa on a safari. The concept had worked successfully in other places, and there was no reason to believe it wouldn't also go over well in San Jose. To top it all off, the promoter had incredible credentials. But this animal act bit the dust with a vengeance.

Another time I invested in a law firm that was going to be the H & R Block of the law business. The timing was perfect: The law profession had just been allowed to advertise. But the venture went right into Chapter 11.

It's a little embarrassing to make these public admissions. It looks as though I'm always investing in losers. Even more embarrassing is the fact that it's usually very difficult, if not impossible, to put a finger on exactly what went wrong in each of these debacles.

Sometimes the basic idea, which seemed so great when we talked about it, was only good as an idea. It didn't have the horsepower to make it in the marketplace. More often the problem was in the execution. The main movers in the company just weren't willing to put in that extra ounce of effort, that additional push to perfection, to get the thing off the ground. They ran into some problems, and then they gave up too soon. Or they were a little too inefficient in overseeing how the seed money was being employed.

I just recently went into a brand-new company that looked like a sure winner. The idea was to offer low-cost delivery of medical services in shopping centers—a kind of around-the-clock medical service station. I knew the principals well and respected their business acumen. Overall, I was really enthusiastic about the project, and we fully anticipated that the company would quickly go public and sell shares for twenty-five times the price we had paid for them.

But unexpected snags developed. The people in charge spent all the money we had put into the company on legal fees, accounting fees, and prospectuses. The new issue bubble in 1983 popped. In 1984 the company filed for bankruptcy and liquidation.

In this "deuces wild" game, what are the indispensable ingredients for success? Astute management, obviously, but that's far from enough. You also must have a lot of timing and, much as I hate to say it, *a lot of luck.*

There are so many possibilities when you try to decide what to do with that 5 percent or so in your portfolio that you've set aside for speculation. Even if you don't make any money on any wild scheme, however, you can have a lot of fun. You may even learn something you never knew before.

For instance, what about windmills? Yes, windmills. Wind power. I investigated this concept recently and regretfully concluded that there is a real problem with them if you hope to turn them into a substitute for the local power plant. They may be appropriate in some geographical areas where the winds blow at near-gale force all the time, but not in downtown Los Angeles or New York.

Still, I got a lot of fresh air and learned some things I never knew about this ancient power source before I turned toward other possibilities. Perhaps if I had been more of an engineering expert, I could have seen some of the special properties of this investment. But I'm not, so I didn't.

Another field that requires a "special handling" sticker is what's called *arbitrage.* This is a catchall term that may include a number of different approaches to investing in certain securities to take advantages of changes and differences in price.

For example, some arbitrageurs (the guys who wheel and deal in arbitrage situations) specialize in companies they expect will get involved in mergers. A merger always affects a company's stock, often driving it up.

I have a friend who reports very good luck in investing through a limited partnership that deals in this merger type of arbitrage. He put a small portion of his portfolio into this vehicle about six years ago, and it's been increasing at the rate of about 30 percent a year. His investment has more than quintupled!

My friend, by the way, is free to admit he doesn't have the foggiest notion about what is going on. He was ready to lose his money, if necessary, but the concept was presented to him by an investment counselor he had reason to trust. Also, the person who was running the arbitrage deal had a string of successes in this type of investment, so he decided to take a flyer, and he lucked out. There we are, back to perhaps the major ingredient of a successful speculation—luck.

In any form of investment exotica the trick is to find someone who has achieved a fine track record with a particular specialty. Then you might put a *small sum* of money into the venture. There may be a steep fee to get into the deal, that's often par for the course in speculation. And if you hit it, the rewards could be very steep on the up side.

I have another friend who has invested in billboards in a limited partnership that proved rather successful. He received 15 percent annual interest on his investment for about two years; he also got some tax write-offs because of the fact that the billboards have the advantages of other real estate ventures; and he got an extra 10 percent on his investment, along with all his initial capital, when he decided to pull out of the deal early.

But I've seen too many fellows hit it lucky on their first play, then load up everything they own on their second play and see it all go down the drain. And there is no third play.

Such ventures don't further a sound, long-term investment program, but they can help you let off steam. As long as you stay in strict control of the amount of capital you're committing, they can provide an invigorating sense of newness, the kind of adventure and excitement all of us relish.

But the important thing to remember, whenever the spice and

excitement begin to get out of hand, is: Making money the old-fashioned but surefooted way is just hard work. It takes time; it takes discipline; it takes patience; and sometimes it's dull as the dickens. But for the large majority of those who hope to achieve reasonable investment goals, the old-fashioned way is the only way.

23

Form Your Own Family
of Stockbrokers

My FATHER, a lawyer with an interest in the stock market, gave me my first understanding of investing when I was about thirteen. He showed me the stock page of the newspaper and said, "These things go up and down."

So I started following a couple of them. I'd select one and say, "Dad, I'd like you to get this for me." He'd nod and go back to his paper. You see, I didn't actually buy at that time, but often one of my mental bets would go up and might even double or triple in a relatively short time.

"Gee," I thought, "this is my kind of game."

This yo-yo effect immediately fascinated me, and I began to look for something that I could afford. I think what I finally settled on was a $1 or 50-cent stock.

So for a long time thereafter I zealously tracked the market. And a couple of years ago I revived the old family tradition with my oldest son, who was then sixteen. I got him interested with some advice on several companies. Then the worst thing happened, similar to what had happened with me. All of them went up in value, and I think he got a bit of a warped view of the market. He decided it was a pushover.

I decided to teach him a lesson. I actually bought him some shares in two high-tech, high-growth companies, and I told him to pick a third on his own. He chose Chrysler, then deep in the dumps. This was twenty years after my first run-in with Chrysler, and I suppose I should have known better than to express any opinion at all. But I didn't.

"Come on!" I protested. "That company is almost bankrupt."

"No," he insisted. "I really want to buy it." So he did, with money he had earned himself.

His reasoning? It wasn't exactly a textbook investment analysis. He just decided that the price was very low, the name sounded familiar, and he could afford to buy a lot of shares—a common mistake, incidentally, among novice investors who mistake quantity for quality.

But my son lucked out. Chrysler, Lee Iacocca at the helm, soared from $3 to $30, and his $100 investment went up ten times, much better than the stocks I had advised him to buy. Now he has the bug. His high school is one of the very few that offers any kind of an investment course, and he took it. Now nineteen, he's in college studying economics.

It's been obvious in my family, and I know others have had the same experience, that exposing youngsters to some of the principles and practicalities of investing at a young age can get them off on a sound financial foot. In fact, I urge that you, too, give your whole family the opportunity to become a family of independent stockbrokers. That means husbands, wives, widows, widowers, mothers-in-law, kids of every age, and even the pets, if they're interested.

But how do you establish a workable strategy for pulling the entire family into a more responsible approach to investments and personal finances? I'd suggest that you begin working with family members one at a time. Here are some considerations for a number of different individuals.

THE RELUCTANT SPOUSE

Traditionally, it's been the wife who hasn't been particularly interested in the stock market, but these days the shoe may well be on the other foot: The husband may be the financially hesitant spouse.

Probably, the problem with the noninvesting spouse is that he or she is afraid of what he or she doesn't understand. To win the resister over, I suggest that you take the following steps:

- Introduce her to the financial pages of your newspaper, especially *The Wall Street Journal,* which carries many popular articles that will catch anyone's interest.
- Buy a no-load fund in his name and persuade him to monitor it on the market pages. You might use this as an opportunity to strike up a casual discussion about diversification (no, I'm not putting you on!).
- Ask him to read some of the more outrageous lines from this book.
- Impress on her how essential it is to understand the family's financial picture in case of your untimely death. In the inspired words of one financial writer, do all you can to "teach your wife to become a widow."

TAKING YOUR MOTHER TO MARKET

This is a toughie because moms don't usually like to kowtow to advice from their kids. But the chances are that she'll become a widow, if she's not one already, since statistically husbands die years before their wives.

One of the unhappiest things I have seen as a professional broker and money manager is that many widows undergo a very frightening experience. They often don't understand much about their investments or security positions, and many of them end up falling prey to very aggressive, smooth-talking brokers who can con them right out of their earnings. It all starts with those assets that the brokers quickly convert into personal income for themselves through commissions. I've seen so many flagrant abuses of this nature.

Let me tell you about one shocking case that has resulted in a $10-million civil suit against a broker with one of the country's best-known, most respected national securities firms named as a codefendant.

Both the broker and the firm have denied any wrongdoing, and the litigation has not yet been resolved. So, in all fairness to them, I won't publicly identify them. But the reported facts are as follows: A relative of one of the alleged victims has openly charged that to support an "extravagant life-style," the broker switched securities merely to reap commissions. Also, he placed funds into high-risk margin accounts. The plaintiffs are two elderly sisters and the daughter of one of the women. One of the three purportedly has been reduced from being able to afford a mansion and chauffeured limousine to working as a maid. The charges in the case include fraud, negligence, and violations of the 1934 Securities Exchange Act.

Even with the potential for serious abuses, it's still often quite hard to get through to that elderly relative of yours. And it's especially hard if they've already established a pleasant relationship with an amiable young person who also happens to be a hard-charging, full-commission stockbroker. But you might try the following approach if you fear your loved one's assets are in danger:

First: Convince her to take her records to an accountant to get an outside opinion about the state of her finances and investments. Don't be threatening; err on the side of being gentle.

Second: Consult with the accountant and then determine whether you can take care of the matter yourself, or whether you need to retain legal counsel.

Third: Begin feeding pertinent financial information to her, such as financial stories with appropriate underlinings, about practices such as the churning of accounts and other abuses by brokers.

Fourth: Enlist another family member or close friend to keep in touch with her as well. Often, if two people are giving similar advice, that has considerably more weight than just one.

Fifth: Steer her to a bank trust department. The stockbroker, whose only compensation is commission and turnover, *should* watch over the account as a fiduciary; but he won't because he doesn't get any compensation for that. The bank, on the other hand, will offer investment or advisory services and will review her account regularly.

Sixth: Help her determine her income needs, and give her some guidance about how she can get into a solid no-load income or bond fund.

Seventh: Don't push her. Let her develop some market expertise and independence at her own pace. Finally, at every stage of the process, show her plenty of understanding and love. After all, it was a need for that which probably got her entangled with that smooth-talking broker in the first place.

KIDS AND CASH

The most interested and pleasingly unpredictable investors in your family are likely to be the children. Give them a little cash, and they'll try to become market magnates overnight. The experience will be fun and may also be a little frustrating, but the education the youngsters will get will be far more than anything they can expect in a classroom.

I know one lawyer who set up an account with a broker for his oldest son, who was only nine or ten years old at the time. Then he gave the boy an open-ended ability to choose securities, though a limited amount of starting capital.

The boy immediately picked some ice cream stocks, and he avidly follows the market now, even though it's three years later.

He periodically gets on the phone to put in an order with his broker, and he sounds just like any seasoned adult investor, except for his soprano voice, which still hasn't changed.

As for my own family, I introduced my youngest son to the stock page at the age of seven. Even at that stage kids are very curious. And when they reach their early teens, that's the time to urge them to look at the financial pages, after they've exhausted the comics and TV listings.

In my own childhood, I also remember I loved to play Monopoly. It's a great game for youngsters to absorb painlessly some basic financial lessons. Today, there are also a number of computer programs that deal with money and financial issues.

But I believe it's absolutely essential for parents eventually to help their children jump feet first into actual investing in the stock market, as that lawyer I described above did. When your child is in her early teens, you might buy ten or twenty shares of a couple of moderately priced securities. It would also be a good idea to introduce her to the concept of no-load mutual funds.

These investments won't involve a lot of money, and they will provide a good vehicle for her to learn about the workings of the market. There's nothing like making a personal commitment with her own real money to hold a child's attention!

TURNING THE FAMILY INTO AN INVESTMENT TEAM

Right now a doctor in Michigan, an attorney in Texas, an investment adviser in Florida, and goodness knows how many other people in other states are operating as independent investors *right out of their own homes*.

Personal computers are emerging as a key tool to transform families from separate individuals into a smoothly working investment team. They allow you to track your investment and cash positions more efficiently, and they can serve as focal points around which the family can gather to discuss common financial concerns.

Very shortly you will be able to obtain all the information about your account from your discount brokers. If you link into a brokerage house with an asset management account, such as Merrill Lynch CMA or Schwab One, you'll also be able to track all your check transactions. Managing your tax situations will also be within the touch of a few keys on your computer.

There's been an explosion of various kinds of financial information services, including software that enables you to manage every aspect of your personal budget and investments. The personal computer is becoming the key to galvanizing family investment planning. It's the very foundation on which you'll be able to form a family of independent stockbrokers.

In my home, we have an Apple; other families may go for an IBM, a Wang or a Radio Shack; but whatever you choose, do it sooner rather than later. A sound family investment strategy begins at home, and a personal computer is one of the best means to get everyone thinking creatively, and in concert, about the movements of the markets.

24

Okay, I'm Ready
to Open an Account!

Now, it's time for you and your interested family members to make some concrete moves into the stock market. It's relatively easy to read about how to do it. But when it comes to rising out of your chair, walking over to the phone, and dialing the number of a real-life brokerage house—well, that's a different matter. In fact, those first steps in opening a new account and executing an actual order can be downright nerve-racking.

What I want to do here is to take you by the hand and lead you point-by-point through the process of opening an account. In fact, you might even want to have the book open at these pages as you experience this new adventure. That way, I'll in effect be accompanying you from start to finish.

These steps, by the way, apply more to setting up an account and executing orders with a discount broker than with a full-commission broker. If you *do* decide to use a full-commission fellow, then the best rule of thumb is, "Sit back, let him do the driving, and keep a close vigilance!"

But if you've decided to go the independent route and make

your own decisions, the following procedures should help you get the best use out of your discount broker.

Step 1: Screw up your courage to open an account. You would be surprised at how hard it is for many people to take action initiating a brokerage account, especially a brand-new brokerage relationship. Or perhaps you wouldn't be surprised. A friend of mine was describing how reluctant he was to go into a brokerage office or even call a broker on the phone. His brow typically broke out in beads of perspiration because he was afraid he was going to sound stupid or make some irreparable mistake.

Of course, the anticipation is far more painful than the actual experience. All you have to do is contact a discount broker in one of three ways: 1) Call him or her up on the telephone. About 60 percent of our customers initially get in touch with us this way. Just find the number in the phone book and dial. 2) Write to the broker. About 20 percent of our people start out this way. 3) Go into the brokerage office. Another 20 percent of our clients kick off their discount brokerage accounts this way, and it is the quickest approach to opening an account if you want to get off the starting blocks in a hurry. The telephone route is the next fastest, while the post office is the slowest.

When you make this first contact, all you have to do is ask the brokerage office to send you brochures describing various brokerage accounts, and also the appropriate application forms. That's it. Then, you wait for the literature, look it over when it arrives, and send in your application to get yourself on the broker's records.

Step 2: Decide how you want to invest. If you're just starting out, you'll undoubtedly want to buy something—probably a no-load growth stock mutual fund. After reading this book or other relevant investment material, you'll be ready to rise out of your chair again and take some additional action. This time, making that contact will be easier than it was before.

Step 3: Invest. Let's say you've decided you want to buy a no-load fund. In that event, you'll have to put enough money into your newly opened account to cover the cost of the shares you plan to buy. Then, you either call, write, or go in personally to the brokerage office. About 5 percent of our investors come into our office, and another 95 percent call in their orders by phone. Almost nobody uses the mail because of the delays.

When you place your order, the brokerage office will want several key pieces of information: your name and account number, the name of the fund or other securities you want to buy, and the amount of money you plan to invest.

Investments other than mutual funds have other requirements as to the amount of money that has to be in your account. For example, if you buy ordinary common stocks, you'll have five business days to pay up. Or if you want to purchase an option, you'll have to have your money in your account at the time of the order, as you do with a mutual fund. Your brokerage house or the literature it puts out will describe the specific requirements for buying or selling different types of investments.

Step 4: Look for a verbal confirmation of your order. As soon as your order has been executed, or completed, by the broker, he'll call to let you know what has happened. Usually, the call will come within an hour. Jot down what he says so that you can use it during Step 5.

Step 5: Watch for written confirmation of your order. Within two business days, you'll get a slip from the brokerage house describing exactly what has happened in the transaction. The written confirmation should match what you were told over the phone.

Step 6: Watch for a reflection of the transaction on your next monthly statement from the brokerage house. Your monthly statement, which is typically mailed out during the first week of each month, should present a comprehensive picture of what has happened in your account during the previous month. All your securities should be listed, along with transactions you've completed during the last month. Be sure to check all the transactions described on this statement to be sure they are consistent with the other confirmations you've received in Steps 4 and 5.

Also, if you have a comprehensive "all-in-one" asset management account, you'll see things on your monthly statement like the amount of margin (or borrowing power) you have available, the interest you've earned on money market instruments, and a list of any checks you may have written if you have check writing privileges.

You may feel a little intimidated initially, as you move from armchair investing to active buying and selling on the market. The first time can be an emotional, unnerving experience for many people, so don't think you're the Lone Ranger. But believe me, after you've done it once, the next time is a piece of cake! The hardest part is just taking that first step into new and exciting territory.

25

Some Random Schwabian Thoughts on the Specter of Inflation

WHEN I think of inflation, what comes to mind is the slumbering Gulliver being tied down by a gaggle of Lilliputians: harmless now, but if it awakens, it will surely break loose from our puny restraints. So we must brace ourselves for this threat to all our planning and prepare damage control measures.

The inflation rate has been fluctuating around 4 to 5 percent per year, and that's pretty good. Perhaps, we'll be able to maintain that level, but if the rate increases much, all the targets for the various age groups and life-cycle stages we spelled out a number of chapters back will have to be increased substantially.

What is the value of the dollar going to be a decade from now? Even if inflation were only 3 percent per annum, over a ten-year period it would add more than 30 percent to your investment objectives. That is, if you thought that you needed to save $10,000, with only 3 percent inflation, you'd better up that target amount to well over $13,000.

But what's the future outlook for inflation? Will the bad Gulliver burst through his bonds and wreak havoc on our economy once again? I think not, at least not for an extended period of time. Although we must never relax our vigilance against this cancerous threat, there seem to me to be two compelling reasons why we will stay in an inflationary rate below 5 percent, and maybe even in the 2 to 3 percent range.

First of all, the political facts of life demand it. Typically, except for periods when we have been at war, the American system gravitates toward a relatively low-inflation economy.

Also, with the deregulation of the financial industry, banks included, the financial markets will be more in equilibrium. With that will come lower inflation. There should be less of the boom-and-bust kind of environment, much of which was fostered by too much government intervention in the economy. I think we've learned something since the sixties, and the result should be a lower, more stable inflation rate.

Some would argue that the size of the federal deficit practically demands a much higher inflation rate in the near future—and, certainly, a $200-billion deficit is not an unimportant number—but I think there has been an exaggerated amount of wheel-spinning and huffing and puffing on the subject. For one thing, the internal creation of savings now is at a very high rate among both individuals, companies, and retirement funds. As a result we are able to create enough savings within the economy to pay for the deficit. I must say that I do hope the deficit can be reduced, because it will always contribute to inflation, but a $200-billion deficit in a $3-*trillion* economy seems manageable to me.

Even as I glibly drop these optimistic observations, however, I want to deliver some sterner warnings out of the other side of my mouth. All age groups should maintain an eternal vigilance against inflation as they plan their portfolios. This is particularly important for those in their fifties and older.

Real estate and growth securities, such as a good no-load mutual fund, seem to be the more promising hedges against any future inflation. Also, they will most likely give you good appreciation, regardless of the inflation rate. So I would be sure to get these properties into my portfolio. Income-producing securities are important for all age groups, but don't put all your money into them, no matter how old you are. If high inflation does once again surface the fixed-income securities will be the first to suffer.

Here's a way to look at the problem when you're planning your portfolio: When you balance off inflation against the rate of return on an investment, if the inflation rate is outrunning the rate of return, you have problems. Clearly, you're losing money. If the two rates, inflation and investment appreciation, just balance out, you are not getting any return on your money. At this writing, even if you put your money into a 9 percent interest-bearing fund and take out 3 to 4 percent for inflation, you are going to end up with only a 6 percent *real* annual return. This might seem acceptable to some people, but not to me!

I say that you must target yourself for higher rates of return, and that means getting a significant portion of your portfolio, at least about a third, into growth securities. If the inflation rate picks up, you in turn must increase your expected return. Always try to set as a minimum an 8 to 10 percent rate of *real* return.

Think about it this way: Assume a gross rate of return of 12 percent on your investments. What happens after ten, twenty, or thirty years, when you get ready to retire? If inflation has held to 2 percent, that's wonderful; you'll be in good shape and may even be able to retire to Florida. But what if it soars up into double digits again? You'll need a wheelbarrow to carry the worthless money of the future—if you can afford a wheelbarrow after all you've lost in real dollars on your investments—just to buy one week's vacation in the Sunshine State.

As I say, I don't expect such a sad scenario. But it's always best to prepare for the worst, even as you fully expect the best.

26

The Ultimate Goal:
Becoming an Investment Sage

IF you've made it this far and you're still as enthusiastic as ever about the investment markets, I consider you a promising candidate for the degree of Investment Sage from the old School Of Hard Knocks (SOHK).

Do not take this honor lightly. It assumes that you have learned *and* put into practice the four keystones of successful independent investing. In descending order, they are:

- Self-discipline
- Flexibility
- Imagination
- Courage

You might also throw in one wild card—luck. And, for good measure, assume you have earned a double degree, the second being a Masters in Market Psychology.

To the Investment Sage, however, *self-discipline* is where it all begins and ends. A paraphrase of one of Kiplings's greatest poems sums it all up: If you can keep your head when all about you are losing theirs and blaming it on you, then you're a Sage, my friend.

Self-discipline enables the Sage to buck the tide: to buy when the panicky are selling and to sell when the euphoric are buying. He makes his decisions coolly, never in the heat of the moment, and he moves on facts, not emotions.

By contrast, the second keystone, *flexibility*, limbers up the Investment Sage's gray matter so that he can quickly reverse course, contravene yesterday's plan to make his strategy conform with today's market conditions. As the market changes, and it frequently does with breathtaking speed, he has the capacity to change with it.

Next to 100-proof stupidity, which unfortunately is not uncommon among investors, *in*flexibility causes the greatest number of disasters among investors who insist on holding on to that dog that can't be revived in a lifetime. Very commendable for dog-lovers, but very silly for investors.

Certainly, every time I found some *absolute* rule about the stock market, I very quickly discovered that it was not a sound principle after all. The market is one of the most humbling places on this earth.

Any Investment Sage who plays golf will quickly appreciate an analogy between his sport and the market. As a kid I played a lot of competitive golf, and I worked hard at my game. I'd go out one day and shoot par; then I'd go out the next day with all the confidence in the world that I'd go under par. Sound reasonable? Of course not! All of a sudden I would skyrocket up to eight or ten above par. One day my putting might be absolutely great and my long game horrible. Then, suddenly, both of these would click at the same time—but my sand shots were just awful.

In golf or the market, the trick is putting it all together at the same time. You can accomplish that by keeping at it month after month and year after year, by constantly expecting the unexpected and changing with the unforeseen. Always, the Investment Sage keeps his options open; he keeps diversified; he stays flexible.

Now, to the third keystone, *imagination*. The wise president of one of the biggest advertising agencies in the country has ticked off what lack of imagination has cost three major industries in the United States:

Newspapers: Back in the 1920s they failed to recognize they were in the communications business and not just the print business. As a result they missed the significance of radio and failed to take over the field; and they've been fighting the "talking box" ever since.

Railroads: When first faced with competition from trucks, they should have asked, "Are we just in railroads or in *transportation?*" You guessed it. They missed it, and much of the freight business as well.

Hollywood: When the first TV appeared, the movie moguls should have seen it as part of the broader entertainment picture and taken over the action. They should have been thinking big, but they thought small. Now, they are suffering for it.

The Investment Sage learns not to make such mistakes. He strives always to see the big picture, not the little individual strokes. By expanding his vision toward infinity, he is always receptive to new ideas, no matter how cockeyed they may seem at first glance. Consequently, he has a good chance to see beyond current investments and fathom where the fortunes of the future will most likely be made.

The fourth keystone of successful independent investing is *courage.* Here, the Investment Sage borrows a word of advice from the professional gambler: "Scared money never wins." He has his own nerves-of-steel definition of a low market: That is the time to buy. Without flinching, he will take a bath in a loser and dump it fast, rather than timidly hold it for years, hoping for a comeback that never comes.

His basic philosophy is best summed up in a slogan coined by Fiorello La Guardia, a former mayor of New York in the halcyon days of the Big Apple: "Patience and fortitude," La Guardia preached, especially when things seem most overcast.

How long will it take to perfect those four keystones of successful Sagedom? You may as well ask how long does it take to perfect a golf swing or a tennis stroke? Each of us marches at a different pace. But the one thing I do know is that, with application, it *will* come. Suddenly the light switches on and everything becomes clear. When you've put in your time and paid your dues, you'll eventually achieve investment maturity.

Of course, on your way to the top of Market Mountain you'll make plenty of mistakes. Just don't make the biggest mistake of all by holding back, by hesitating to take a chance on what looks like the right investment at the right time.

All that matters, after you've taken your knocks and learned what the past has to teach, is to fix your sights on the future. For the Investment Sage, the past must, in the final analysis, become "a bucket of ashes," in Carl Sandburg's memorable phrase. Your fortune lies in the future and thus your outlook must be one of optimism, of expectation.

Back in the Great Depression days, Investment Sages defiantly sang "Who's Afraid of the Big Bad Wolf?" Similarly, there has been an amusing but also gallant tradition on the New York Stock Exchange to throw off the gloom at the close of a disastrous day. From somewhere among the crowd of silent, dejected traders a voice would rise in song, and soon dozens and dozens more would join in, roaring out that golden oldie, "Wait Till the Sun Shines, Nellie"!

That might well be the theme song for today's Investment Sage. No matter how dark the passing clouds, he knows that he *will* find that sunshine once again.

Appendix:
The Charles Schwab No-Load
Mutual Fund Marketplace

To indicate the wide range of no-load mutual funds that are available, the following lists more than 200 mutual funds traded through Charles Schwab & Co., Inc. This information is dated as of January 1, 1986, and will change substantially over time.

Historical financial data was provided by DAL Investment Co., a registered investment advisor and publisher of the monthly newsletter **No Load Fund* X. For more information: 235 Montgomery Street, Dept. 838S, San Francisco, CA 94104, (415) 986-7979.

How to read this listing:

Fund name. Funds are listed alphabetically within the following categories: Aggressive Growth • Growth • Growth & Income • Option/Income • Income • Balanced • Special Purpose • Tax-Exempt Income • Bond

Year first offered. The first year the fund was made available to the public.

Total return. The total return of the fund, calculated with dividends and capital gains reinvested at the end of the periods shown.

Yield %. The percentage yield, based upon dividends paid, for the one-year period ending the date shown.

FUND NAME	FIRST YEAR OFFERED	------TOTAL RETURN PERCENTAGE CHANGES------				YIELD% Annual Div to 12/31/85
		BEAR MARKET 8/14/81– 8/13/82	BULL MARKET 7/13/84– 7/12/85	5 Yr to 6/30/85 %	1 Yr to 12/31/85 %	

AGGRESSIVE GROWTH FUNDS

FUND NAME	FIRST YEAR OFFERED	BEAR MARKET 8/14/81–8/13/82	BULL MARKET 7/13/84–7/12/85	5 Yr to 6/30/85 %	1 Yr to 12/31/85 %	YIELD% Annual Div to 12/31/85
American Investors Fund, Inc.	1958	-55.5 %	5.3 %	-7.4 %	14.2 %	2.5 %
Bull & Bear Capital Growth Fund	1960	-28.4	28.6	73.6	27.3	0.8
Dividend/Growth Laser & Adv Tech	1983	n.a.	n.a.	n.a.	0.3	0.0
Dreyfus Growth Opportunity Fund	1972	-33.1	14.2	41.3	29.4	1.8
Fidelity Freedom Fund, Inc.	1982	n.a.	29.7	n.a.	28.6	1.5
Fidelity Magellan Fund, Inc. #	1963	-8.0	42.4	213.2	41.4	1.4
Fidelity Mercury Fund, Inc. #	1983	n.a.	38.6	n.a.	39.7	0.4
Fidelity OTC Portfolio #	1985	n.a.	n.a.	n.a.	59.1	0.1
Fidelity Select Portfolios, Inc. #						
Brokerage & Investment Mgmt	1985	n.a.	n.a.	n.a.	n.a.	n.a.
Chemicals	1985	n.a.	n.a.	n.a.	n.a.	n.a.
Computers	1985	n.a.	n.a.	n.a.	n.a.	n.a.
Defense & Aerospace	1984	n.a.	31.2	n.a.	26.3	0.7
Electronics	1985	n.a.	n.a.	n.a.	n.a.	n.a.
Energy	1981	n.a.	16.2	n.a.	18.1	5.7
Financial Services	1981	n.a.	62.3	n.a.	40.9	1.0
Food & Agriculture	1985	n.a.	n.a.	n.a.	n.a.	n.a.
Health Care	1981	n.a.	67.8	n.a.	59.4	0.2
Leisure & Entertainment	1984	n.a.	66.4	n.a.	56.4	0.1
Precious Metals & Minerals	1981	n.a.	-7.9	n.a.	-9.8	4.6
Software & Computer Services	1985	n.a.	n.a.	n.a.	n.a.	n.a.
Technology	1981	n.a.	4.4	n.a.	7.2	1.8
Telecommunications	1985	n.a.	n.a.	n.a.	n.a.	n.a.
Utilities	1981	n.a.	49.2	n.a.	31.4	2.2
Fidelity Special Situations #	1983	n.a.	34.0	n.a.	36.7	1.6

Low-load funds. <>Fund is currently closed to new accounts.
n.a. means the fund was not in existence the full time period described

| FUND NAME | FIRST YEAR OFFERED | TOTAL RETURN PERCENTAGE CHANGES | | | | YIELD% Annual Div to 12/31/85 |
		BEAR MARKET 8/14/81–8/13/82 %	BULL MARKET 7/13/84–7/12/85 %	5 Yr to 6/30/85 %	1 Yr to 12/31/85 %	
Financial Strategic Portfolios						
Energy	1984	n.a.	n.a.	n.a.	13.5	1.9
Gold	1984	n.a.	n.a.	n.a.	-4.4	2.6
Health Sciences	1984	n.a.	n.a.	n.a.	31.4	0.1
Leisure	1984	n.a.	n.a.	n.a.	32.2	0.4
Pacific Basin	1984	n.a.	n.a.	n.a.	27.3	0.0
Technology	1984	n.a.	n.a.	n.a.	27.4	0.0
Founders Special Fund, Inc.	1960	-25.4	20.0	95.7	15.2	1.0
Gintel Capital Appreciation Fund	1985	n.a.	n.a.	n.a.	n.a.	n.a.
Hartwell Leverage Fund	1968	-34.0	16.5	62.9	27.0	0.9
Janus Fund, Inc.	1970	-6.3	23.4	141.0	24.5	3.9
Janus Venture Fund, Inc.	1985	n.a.	n.a.	n.a.	n.a.	0.0
Lehman Capital Fund	1976	-5.1	19.8	115.6	23.0	0.9
Lehman Opportunity Fund	1979	-20.3	38.3	131.4	32.5	1.8
Omega Fund	1968	-40.9	40.8	34.7	32.1	0.8
Pacific Horizon Aggressive Growth	1984	n.a.	n.a.	n.a.	37.5	0.3
Quest for Value Fund, Inc.	1980	5.3	n.a.	237.1	26.8	1.1
T.Rowe Price New Horizons Fund	1960	-25.1	17.2	83.5	23.5	0.9
Scudder Capital Growth Fund	1957	-12.2	36.1	112.0	35.1	1.3
Scudder Development Fund, Inc.	1971	-17.1	15.9	96.6	19.4	0.8
Sherman, Dean Fund, Inc.	1968	-46.4	-3.8	-27.3	11.4	0.6
SteinRoe & Farnham Cap. Opprtn.	1963	-29.3	16.7	65.9	24.4	1.2
SteinRoe Special Fund, Inc.	1968	-20.2	34.3	130.0	28.6	1.0
Value Line Leveraged Growth	1972	-5.8	37.5	82.1	27.0	0.6
Value Line Special Situations	1956	-17.2	12.8	71.6	23.1	0.3
Vanguard Explorer Fund <>	1967	-17.5	10.6	113.4	22.2	0.9
Vanguard Explorer II	1985	n.a.	n.a.	n.a.	n.a.	0.4
Vanguard Naess & Thomas Special	1959	-17.4	7.8	81.9	21.1	1.0
Vanguard Specialized Portfolios						
Energy	1984	n.a.	n.a.	n.a.	14.3	1.3
Gold & Precious Metals	1984	n.a.	-7.0	n.a.	-5.0	0.9
Health Care	1984	n.a.	50.0	n.a.	45.2	0.5
Service Economy	1984	n.a.	52.2	n.a.	43.3	0.5
Technology	1984	n.a.	12.2	n.a.	13.9	0.4

GROWTH FUNDS

FUND NAME	FIRST YEAR OFFERED	BEAR MARKET 8/14/81–8/13/82 %	BULL MARKET 7/13/84–7/12/85 %	5 Yr to 6/30/85 %	1 Yr to 12/31/85 %	YIELD% Annual Div to 12/31/85
Calvert Fund Equity Portfolio	1982	n.a.	20.2	n.a.	23.3	1.7
Columbia Growth Fund	1967	-14.0	39.3	108.7	31.7	1.2

#Low-load funds. <>Fund is currently closed to new accounts.

n.a. Not available, usually because the fund was not in existence the full time period described.

FUND NAME	FIRST YEAR OFFERED	TOTAL RETURN PERCENTAGE CHANGES				YIELD% Annual Div to 12/31/85
		BEAR MARKET 8/14/81–8/13/82	BULL MARKET 7/13/84–7/12/85	5 Yr to 6/30/85 %	1 Yr to 12/31/85 %	
Dreyfus Fund Incorporated	1947	-14.6	31.2	80.5	23.2	3.3
Dreyfus Third Century Fund, Inc.	1972	-27.2	33.9	35.4	28.6	2.6
Energy Fund, Inc.	1955	-24.1	21.7	44.3	21.6	4.6
Federated Growth Trust	1984	n.a.	n.a.	n.a.	34.1	2.7
Fidelity Contrafund, Inc.	1967	-16.1	27.9	69.6	29.6	2.0
Fidelity Discoverer Fund	1978	-12.3	26.9	115.3	22.1	1.9
Fidelity Trend Fund Inc.	1958	-25.5	27.1	74.7	27.7	1.1
Financial Dynamics Fund, Inc.	1967	-7.1	27.9	70.2	28.9	1.1
Founders Growth Fund, Inc.	1963	-12.4	31.9	97.3	28.8	2.1
Gintel Fund, Inc.	1981	8.2	23.2	n.a.	19.1	1.9
Hartwell Growth Fund	1965	-31.9	15.2	91.1	22.1	0.0
Janus Value Fund, Inc.	1985	n.a.	n.a.	n.a.	n.a.	3.6
Lexington Growth Fund, Inc.	1969	-30.8	32.4	31.6	26.4	1.2
Manhattan Fund, Inc.	1966	-12.6	40.7	141.6	36.7	0.2
Medical Technology Fund, Inc.	1979	-14.0	29.5	86.9	38.9	0.0
Newport Far East Fund	1984	n.a.	n.a.	16.0	16.0	0.0
Partners Fund Incorporated	1968	4.2	31.9	79.2	22.5	3.5
PRO Fund, Inc.	1967	-19.2	29.1	65.4	22.6	2.7
T.Rowe Price Growth Stock Fund	1950	-23.1	35.2	56.8	33.3	1.8
T.Rowe Price New Era Fund	1969	-34.4	23.4	48.0	21.2	3.4
SAFECO Growth Fund Inc.	1967	-23.5	24.4	87.0	18.5	2.3
Selected Special Shares, Inc.	1939	-23.1	21.4	69.1	22.7	1.7
Steinroe & Farnham Stock Fund	1958	-16.7	30.5	68.0	26.3	2.1
United Services Good & Bad Times	1981	-7.2	27.3	n.a.	23.6	1.7
United Services Growth Fund	1983	n.a.	n.a.	n.a.	20.9	0.8
United Services LoCap Fund	1985	n.a.	n.a.	n.a.	n.a.	n.a.
Value Line Fund Inc.	1949	-0.2	33.5	66.4	34.4	1.4
Vanguard W.L. Morgan Growth Fund	1968	-14.6	25.9	90.6	28.1	1.7
Vanguard World Fund						
International Growth Portfolio	1985	n.a.	n.a.	n.a.	n.a.	n.a.
U.S. Growth Portfolio	1985	n.a.	n.a.	n.a.	n.a.	n.a.

GROWTH & INCOME FUNDS

FUND NAME	FIRST YEAR OFFERED	BEAR MARKET 8/14/81–8/13/82	BULL MARKET 7/13/84–7/12/85	5 Yr to 6/30/85 %	1 Yr to 12/31/85 %	YIELD% Annual Div to 12/31/85
Bull & Bear Equity-Income Fund	1961	-6.5	27.2	68.9	22.8	5.5
Century Shares Trust	1928	-9.5	63.7	111.7	40.3	2.8
Dividend/Growth - Dividend Series	1980	14.6	n.a.	93.4	13.2	3.1
Federated Stock Trust	1982	n.a.	42.6	n.a.	32.4	3.1
Federated Stock & Bond Fund, Inc.	1968	2.1	30.8	95.3	22.6	6.2

#Low-load funds. <>Fund is currently closed to new accounts.

n.a. Not available, usually because the fund was not in existence the full time period described.

FUND NAME	FIRST YEAR OFFERED	BEAR MARKET 8/14/81– 8/13/82 %	BULL MARKET 7/13/84– 7/12/85 %	5 Yr to 6/30/85 %	1 Yr to 12/31/85 %	YIELD% Annual Div to 12/31/85
Fidelity Equity-Income Fund #	1975	-1.6	34.0	118.1	24.1	6.1
Fidelity Fund, Inc.	1930	-7.1	30.5	88.7	27.2	4.0
Fidelity Puritan Fund	1947	-0.4	34.0	101.4	26.6	7.1
Financial Industrial Fund, Inc.	1935	-1.6	32.1	47.9	26.3	2.7
Founders Mutual Fund	1982	-16.5	27.2	n.a.	27.7	3.3
Guardian Mutual Fund, Inc.	1950	-11.6	33.8	94.5	23.6	3.8
Ivy Growth Fund	1961	-3.2	33.7	140.3	26.9	5.8
Ivy Institutional Investors <>	1984	n.a.	36.1	n.a.	36.3	3.1
Lehman Investors Fund	1958	-10.2	24.8	94.3	24.4	2.6
Lexington Research Fund, Inc.	1939	-17.6	29.5	65.8	25.8	3.8
Mutual Qualified Income, Inc.	1980	-4.5	20.9	n.a.	25.4	3.2
Mutual Shares Corporation	1949	-11.6	22.4	107.6	26.3	3.8
T.Rowe Price Growth & Income	1982	n.a.	23.8	n.a.	19.2	4.0
SAFECO Equity Fund, Inc.	1932	-19.7	32.5	62.5	31.4	4.3
Scudder Growth & Income Fund	1929	-23.7	41.4	47.2	33.9	3.4
Selected American Shares, Inc.	1933	-3.9	37.1	105.5	32.1	3.8
Stratton Growth Fund, Inc.	1972	-16.8	30.8	122.3	27.1	3.0
Strong Investment Fund, Inc.	1982	n.a.	16.9	n.a.	18.7	1.0
Strong Total Return Fund, Inc.	1982	n.a.	21.8	n.a.	24.4	3.9
Vanguard Index Trust	1976	-16.2	32.4	88.3	30.7	2.9
Vanguard Trustees' Commingled International Equity	1983	n.a.	27.5	n.a.	39.9	3.7
U.S. Equity	1980	-15.1	25.0	88.8	30.2	2.8
Vanguard Windsor Fund <>	1958	-10.2	39.6	122.5	26.2	4.1
Vanguard Windsor Fund II	1985	n.a.	n.a.	n.a.	n.a.	5.2

OPTION/INCOME FUNDS

FUND NAME	FIRST YEAR OFFERED	BEAR MARKET	BULL MARKET	5 Yr	1 Yr	YIELD%
Founders Income Fund	1962	-5.9	19.7	76.7	12.2	5.3

INCOME FUNDS

FUND NAME	FIRST YEAR OFFERED	BEAR MARKET	BULL MARKET	5 Yr	1 Yr	YIELD%
American Investors Income Fund	1976	-13.4	17.9	34.9	21.8	11.6
Benham GNMA Income Fund	1985	n.a.	n.a.	n.a.	n.a.	n.a.
Bull & Bear High Yield Fund	1983	n.a.	24.5	n.a.	19.7	13.2
Capital Preservation Treas. Note	1980	15.9	15.7	47.7	16.9	8.6
Columbia Fixed Income Securities	1983	n.a.	21.2	n.a.	22.7	10.3
Dreyfus GNMA Fund	1985	n.a.	n.a.	n.a.	n.a.	10.0
Federated GNMA Trust	1982	n.a.	25.2	n.a.	18.4	10.3
Federated Income Trust	1982	n.a.	22.9	n.a.	18.7	11.4

#Low-load funds. <>Fund is currently closed to new accounts.

n.a. Not available, usually because the fund was not in existence the full time period described.

| FUND NAME | FIRST YEAR OFFERED | ------TOTAL RETURN PERCENTAGE CHANGES------ | | | | YIELD% |
		BEAR MARKET 8/14/81– 8/13/82	BULL MARKET 7/13/84– 7/12/85	5 Yr to 6/30/85 %	1 Yr to 12/31/85 %	Annual Div to 12/31/85
Federated Intermed. Gov. Trust	1983	n.a.	20.2	n.a.	14.7	10.4
Fidelity Ginnie Mae Portfolio	1985	n.a.	n.a.	n.a.	n.a.	n.a.
Fidelity Mortgage Securities	1985	n.a.	n.a.	n.a.	n.a.	11.0
Financial Industrial Income Fund	1960	2.6	32.1	79.1	28.8	4.8
Lexington GNMA Income Fund	1973	19.9	20.1	36.4	16.1	11.5
Northeast Investors Trust	1950	14.2	31.1	54.5	24.1	11.5
PRO Income Fund, Inc.	1974	14.7	17.8	42.0	17.2	9.2
SAFECO Income Fund, Inc.	1968	-9.0	34.7	99.7	30.4	5.1
Scudder Income Fund, Inc.	1928	10.8	27.5	52.6	20.6	10.1
Stratton Monthly Dividend Shares	1981	-0.5	49.4	n.a.	28.4	8.1
United Services Income	1983	n.a.	n.a.	n.a.	15.1	3.1
Value Line Income Fund, Inc.	1952	8.9	32.4	82.6	22.9	6.8

BALANCED FUNDS

FUND NAME	FIRST YEAR OFFERED	BEAR MARKET 8/14/81– 8/13/82	BULL MARKET 7/13/84– 7/12/85	5 Yr to 6/30/85 %	1 Yr to 12/31/85 %	Annual Div to 12/31/85
Dreyfus Special Income Fund	1971	-6.4	22.2	66.3	22.4	6.3
Pax World Fund, Inc.	1970	-10.4	32.0	72.9	24.1	3.8
SteinRoe Total Return Fund	1949	-12.6	31.4	60.9	24.7	5.6
Vanguard Wellesley Income Fund	1970	4.5	34.2	82.7	26.4	9.0
Vanguard Wellington Fund	1929	-3.0	32.9	89.7	27.7	6.2

SPECIAL PURPOSE FUNDS

FUND NAME	FIRST YEAR OFFERED	BEAR MARKET 8/14/81– 8/13/82	BULL MARKET 7/13/84– 7/12/85	5 Yr to 6/30/85 %	1 Yr to 12/31/85 %	Annual Div to 12/31/85
Bull & Bear Golconda Investors	1974	-26.8	-1.1	-16.7	2.5	1.3
Calvert Social Investment Fund	1982	n.a.	30.8	n.a.	26.0	4.4
Fidelity Overseas Fund #	1984	n.a.	n.a.	n.a.	78.6	0.0
FT International Fund	1984	n.a.	n.a.	n.a.	61.1	0.1
Gintel ERISA Fund, Inc.	1982	n.a.	n.a.	n.a.	22.4	2.7
Lexington GoldFund, Inc.	1979	-27.9	-3.6	-14.9	12.8	1.2
T.Rowe Price International Fund	1980	-19.0	20.4	49.9	42.8	1.6
Scudder International Fund, Inc.	1954	-17.3	23.8	48.9	48.0	1.3
United Services Gold Shares	1974	-21.4	-15.6	16.5	-26.0	7.5
United Services New Prospector	1985	n.a.	n.a.	n.a.	n.a.	n.a.
United Services Prospector Fund◇	1983	-17.9	n.a.	n.a.	0.0	0.0
Value Line Convertible Fund	1985	n.a.	n.a.	n.a.	n.a.	4.2
Vanguard PRIMECAP Fund	1984	n.a.	n.a.	n.a.	35.8	0.1
Vanguard Qualified Dividend						
Portfolio I <>	1975	6.3	45.3	152.6	28.8	6.9
Portfolio II	1975	14.7	35.8	56.7	28.5	10.6
Portfolio III	1983	n.a.	18.0	n.a.	11.3	8.8

#Low-load funds. <>Fund is currently closed to new accounts.
n.a. Not available, usually because the fund was not in existence the full time period described.

FUND NAME	FIRST YEAR OFFERED	TOTAL RETURN PERCENTAGE CHANGES				YIELD% Annual Div to 12/31/85
		BEAR MARKET 8/14/81– 8/13/82	BULL MARKET 7/13/84– 7/12/85	5 Yr to 6/30/85 %	1 Yr to 12/31/85 %	

TAX-EXEMPT FUNDS

FUND NAME	FIRST YEAR OFFERED	BEAR MARKET 8/14/81–8/13/82	BULL MARKET 7/13/84–7/12/85	5 Yr to 6/30/85 %	1 Yr to 12/31/85 %	YIELD% Annual Div to 12/31/85
Benham California Tax-Free Trust						
Intermediate Term	1983	n.a.	14.4	n.a.	13.4	6.9
Long Term	1983	n.a.	19.7	n.a.	17.3	8.1
Benham National Tax-Free Trust						
Intermediate Term	1984	n.a.	n.a.	n.a.	12.1	7.7
Long Term	1984	n.a.	n.a.	n.a.	18.3	8.8
Bull & Bear Tax-Free Income Fund	1985	n.a.	22.7	n.a.	21.5	8.3
Dreyfus Calif. Tax-Exempt Bond	1983	n.a.	18.8	n.a.	17.4	8.0
Dreyfus Insured Tax-Exempt Bond	1985	n.a.	n.a.	n.a.	n.a.	7.2
Dreyfus Intermd. Tax-Exempt Bond	1983	n.a.	16.0	n.a.	15.5	7.8
Dreyfus NY Tax-Exempt Bond	1983	n.a.	19.4	n.a.	19.9	7.9
Dreyfus Tax-Exempt Bond Fund	1976	11.1	20.9	30.1	18.6	8.5
Federated Shrt-Intrmd. Muni.	1981	n.a.	6.9	n.a.	6.4	6.1
Fidelity California Tax-Free						
Municipal Bond	1984	n.a.	16.9	n.a.	15.9	8.6
Short Term	1984	n.a.	5.8	n.a.	4.9	5.0
Fidelity Gov. Securities Fund	1979	20.8	19.6	49.7	16.6	10.1
Fidelity High Yield Muni. Bond	1977	13.3	21.9	36.0	20.5	8.3
Fidelity Limited Term Muni. Bond	1977	11.8	18.3	33.9	16.7	7.1
Fidelity Massachusetts Tax-Free	1983	n.a.	n.a.	n.a.	18.9	8.5
Fidelity Municipal Bond Fund	1976	11.9	20.4	25.2	19.3	7.8
Fidelity New York Free High Yield	1984	n.a.	22.4	n.a.	20.1	8.1
Financial Tax-Free Income Shares	1984	n.a.	22.5	n.a.	21.5	7.9
Nuveen Municipal Bond Fund	1976	7.9	22.5	31.7	20.6	7.0
Pacific Horizon Calif Tax-Exempt	1984	n.a.	21.7	n.a.	17.9	8.1
T.Rowe Price Tax-Free High Yield	1985	n.a.	n.a.	n.a.	n.a.	8.1
T.Rowe Price Tax-Free Income	1976	10.1	12.0	37.7	16.2	7.7
T.Rowe Price Tax-Free Short Intrm	1983	n.a.	9.3	n.a.	8.6	6.3
SAFECO Calif. Tax-Free Income	1983	n.a.	23.8	n.a.	20.4	7.7
SAFECO Municipal Bond Fund	1981	n.a.	23.5	n.a.	20.6	8.3
Scudder California Tax-Free Fund	1983	n.a.	21.5	n.a.	17.8	7.2
Scudder Managed Municipal Bonds	1976	12.9	21.6	33.0	16.9	7.0
Scudder New York Tax-Free Fund	1983	n.a.	19.2	n.a.	15.5	7.2
Scudder Tax-Free Target Fund						
1987 Portfolio	1983	n.a.	10.9	n.a.	7.0	5.8
1990 Portfolio	1983	n.a.	14.1	n.a.	10.7	6.8
1993 Portfolio	1983	n.a.	17.5	n.a.	14.0	7.1

Low-load funds. <> Fund is currently closed to new accounts.

n.a. Not available, usually because the fund was not in existence the full time period described.

FUND NAME	FIRST YEAR OFFERED	TOTAL RETURN PERCENTAGE CHANGES				YIELD% Annual Div to 12/31/85
		BEAR MARKET 8/14/81–8/13/82 %	BULL MARKET 7/13/84–7/12/85 %	5 Yr to 6/30/85 %	1 Yr to 12/31/85 %	
Selected Tax-Exempt Bond Fund	1977	5.6	n.a.	20.3	18.6	7.3
SteinRoe Tax-Exempt Bond Fund	1977	13.8	22.5	41.7	22.1	7.6
Value Line Tax-Exempt Fund, Inc.	1984	n.a.	21.5	n.a.	18.9	9.1
Vanguard Municipal Bond Fund						
High Yield	1978	8.9	21.8	34.7	20.8	8.6
Insured Long-Term	1985	n.a.	n.a.	n.a.	18.6	8.3
Intermediate Term	1977	9.1	18.9	25.1	16.7	8.0
Long Term	1977	9.3	22.1	27.2	20.0	8.4
Short Term	1977	9.3	8.5	35.4	6.8	6.2
BOND FUNDS						
Dreyfus A Bonds Plus, Inc.	1976	18.2	27.5	56.7	21.8	9.8
Federated High Yield Trust	1985	n.a.	n.a.	n.a.	20.6	12.3
Fidelity Corporate Bond Fund	1971	19.5	23.9	43.7	19.8	10.7
Fidelity High Income Fund, Inc.	1977	15.6	28.1	69.8	24.1	12.1
Fidelity Thrift Trust	1975	20.6	25.9	62.6	19.9	10.1
Financial Bond Shares, Inc.						
High Yield Portfolio	1984	n.a.	28.6	n.a.	25.2	12.3
Select Income Portfolio	1976	18.7	22.3	47.7	21.5	10.5
Liberty Fund, Inc.	1956	6.0	25.1	44.0	20.1	7.9
Pacific Horizon High Yield Bond	1984	n.a.	n.a.	n.a.	15.7	12.6
T.Rowe Price High Yield Fund	1984	n.a.	n.a.	n.a.	16.6	12.6
T.Rowe Price New Income Fund	1973	17.2	16.2	45.8	16.6	10.3
T.Rowe Price Short Term Bond Fund	1984	n.a.	14.4	n.a.	12.2	9.1
Scudder Target Fund						
General 1986 Portfolio	1983	n.a.	11.8	n.a.	11.6	6.1
General 1987 Portfolio	1983	n.a.	n.a.	n.a.	14.1	6.8
General 1990 Portfolio	1983	n.a.	10.8	n.a.	17.6	8.0
U.S. Gov't 1986 Portfolio	1983	n.a.	n.a.	n.a.	9.7	5.8
U.S. Gov't 1987 Portfolio	1983	n.a.	25.3	n.a.	12.4	6.7
U.S. Gov't 1990 Portfolio	1983	n.a.	n.a.	n.a.	16.1	7.4
SteinRoe Bond Fund, Inc.	1978	19.0	24.6	42.0	21.4	9.1
Value Line Bond Fund, Inc.	1981	n.a.	28.2	n.a.	19.9	10.0
Vanguard Fixed Income Securities						
GNMA Portfolio	1980	24.4	26.0	n.a.	19.4	10.9
High Yield Portfolio	1978	16.8	23.9	56.1	20.5	13.3
Investment Grade Portfolio	1973	20.9	26.9	52.4	20.5	11.9
Short Term Portfolio	1982	19.7	19.7	n.a.	14.2	9.5
S & P 500 (Including Dividends)		-16.6	33.2	98.6	31.0	3.7
Dow Jones Ind (DJIA)		-10.5	26.1	86.3	32.9	4.1

#Low-load funds. <>Fund is currently closed to new accounts.

Index